THE WORLD CUP

The Photo Record of the Tournament of Surprises

OF **2002**

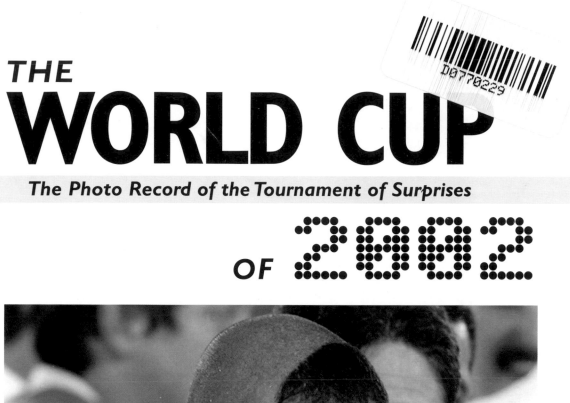

First published in 2002

10 9 8 7 6 5 4 3 2 1

Copyright © 2002 Carlton Books Limited

Carlton Books Limited
20 Mortimer Street
London W1T 3JW

A CIP catalogue record for this book is available from the British Library

ISBN 1 84222 770 X

Written by: Tim Glynne-Jones
Designed by: Cactus Design
Managing Editor: Martin Corteel
Project Art Editors: Mark Lloyd and Jim Lockwood
Project Editors: Nigel Matheson and Martin Richardson
Picture Researcher: Marc Glanville
Production: Sarah Corteel

All pictures courtesy of Empics
Every effort has been made to acknowledge correctly and contact the source and/copyright holder of each picture, and Carlton Books apologises for any unintentional errors or omissions which will be corrected in future editions of this book.

Printed and bound in Great Britain

THE WORLD CUP

The Photo Record of the Tournament of Surprises

OF 2002

Tim Glynne-Jones

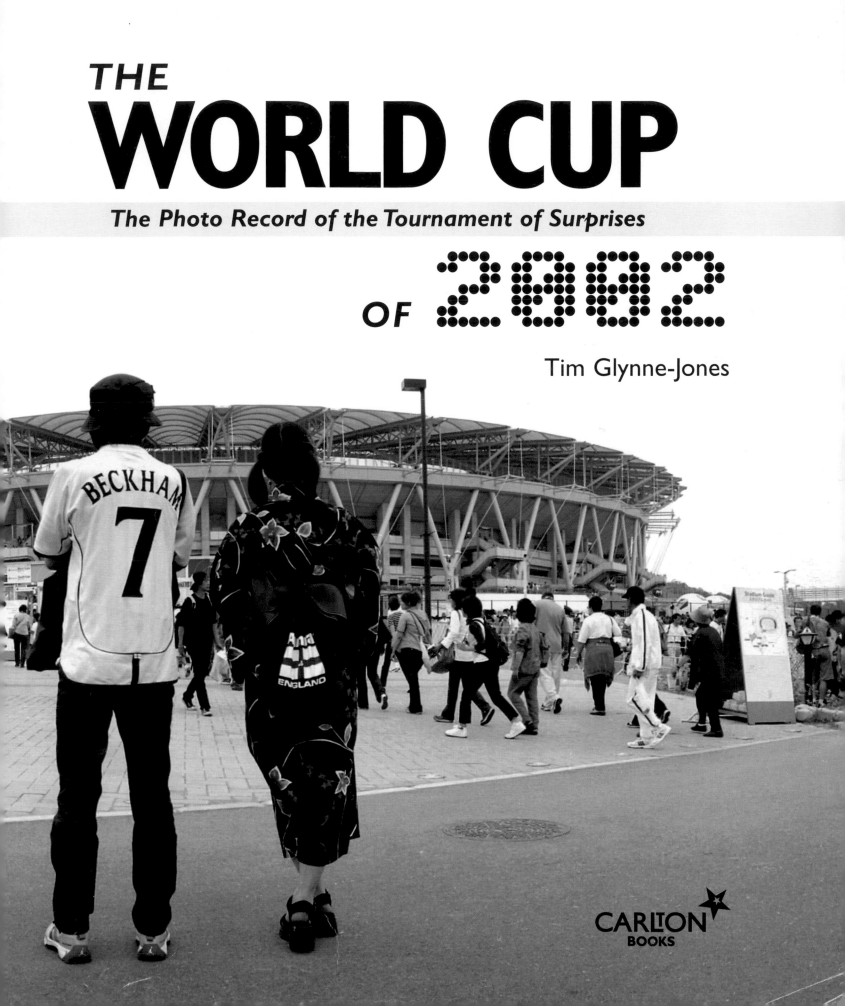

CARLTON BOOKS

CONTENTS

KEY TO MATCH STATS (Group Stages)
● denotes Yellow card   * denotes Red card

HERALDING A NEW AGE

BEFORE A BALL HAD BEEN KICKED Korea/Japan 2002 was already an historic World Cup. Never before had this great tournament been held in Asia and never before had it been shared between co-hosts. The Koreans and Japanese had spent billions of pounds building 19 brand new stadiums to ensure that this World Cup would be a spectacular success and, having invested so heavily off the pitch, they were determined to prove themselves worthy competitors on it, too.

They weren't the only ones. China, Ecuador, Senegal and Slovenia had all qualified for the first time, and were determined to mix it with the big boys of Brazil, Italy, France and Spain. But for all the ground-breaking steps being taken in the build-up to this World Cup, nobody could have foreseen the upheaval that would take place when the games got under way.

The tone was set by Senegal's shock defeat of champions France in the opening match and from that moment on the upsets came thick and fast, so much so that they ceased to be regarded as upsets at all. The co-favourites, Argentina and France, went out in the first round, joined by Portugal. Italy and Spain followed in quick succession in the knock-out stages. Of the traditional giants of the game, only Brazil and Germany, winners seven times between them but both said to be below their customary standard, made it through to the semi-finals.

The old order was changing beyond anybody's expectations and football was truly about to become the world game.

A Japanese fan becomes Brazilian for a month

WELCOME TO SEOUL

While Japan had the honour of hosting the final, South Korea got to stage the opening ceremony in Seoul. And they weren't about to waste the opportunity to put on an eye-catching show in front of a worldwide television audience of 500 million people.

EXOTIC SETTINGS

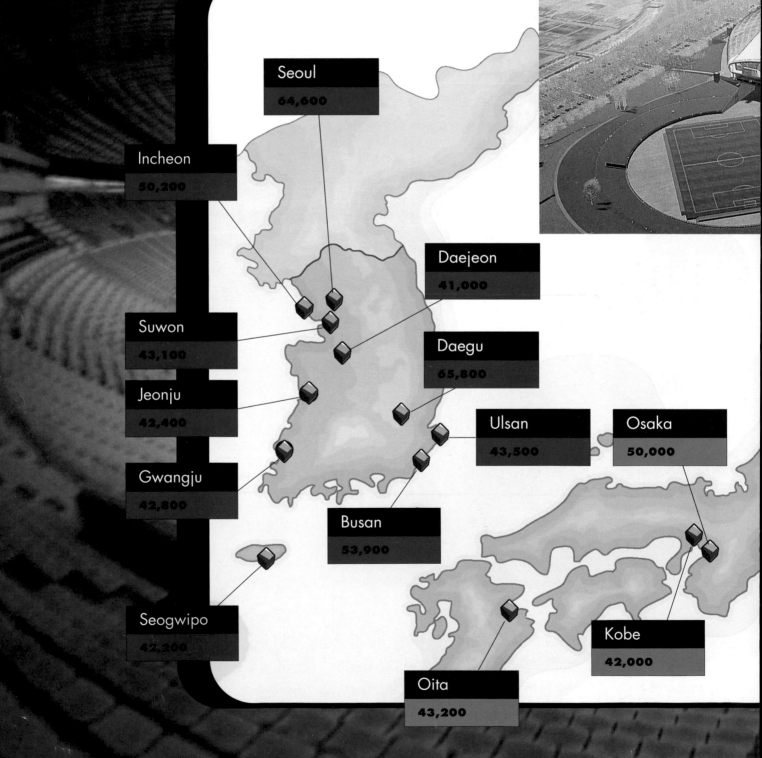

Seoul
64,600

Incheon
50,200

Daejeon
41,000

Suwon
43,100

Daegu
65,800

Jeonju
42,400

Ulsan
43,500

Osaka
50,000

Gwangju
42,800

Busan
53,900

Kobe
42,000

Seogwipo
42,200

Oita
43,200

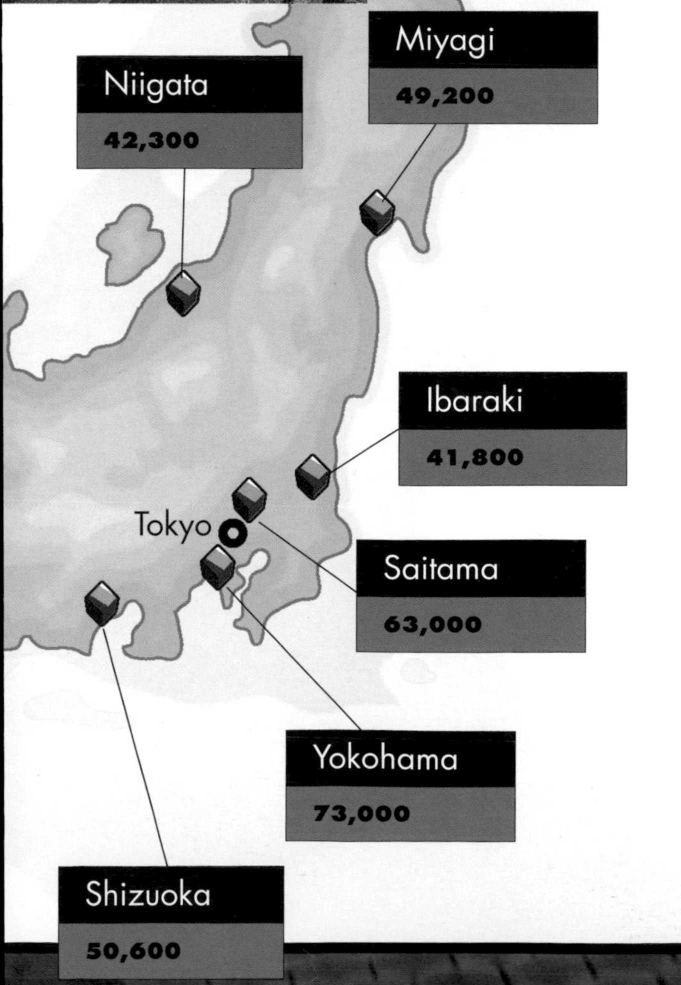

Sapporo

42,300

Miyagi

49,200

Niigata

42,300

Ibaraki

41,800

Tokyo

Saitama

63,000

Yokohama

73,000

Shizuoka

50,600

FOR REASONS KNOWN only to themselves, South Korea and Japan decided to provide 10 stadiums each to host the 64 matches of the World Cup. At a total cost of £4 billion, they set about building 19 of those 20 stadiums from scratch, despite the fact that many of them would only be used for three games.

The stadiums they built became a feature of the tournament, memorable designs combining great beauty with the latest technology. At Sapporo in Japan, the pitch rolled into the stadium on runners and then rotated into position. Saitama was built to be earthquake-resistant with a system that stored rainwater for both the pitch and the toilets. Some had retractable roofs, others were designed to resemble swans, sailing ships and whirlpools. Only Yokohama, the venue for the final, had not been built specially for the World Cup.

Given the local enthusiasm drummed up by the exploits of the South Korea and Japan teams, they may well get regular use in the future, but whatever happens from now on, World Cup 2002 will always be remembered for its exotic venues.

On paper this was the toughest group in the top half of the draw, with Senegal, Denmark and Uruguay all quite evenly placed to claim second place behind hot favourites France. Since becoming champions in 1998, France had added a world class strike force to their armoury and were expected to go all the way. But on the eve of the tournament, their star player Zinedine Zidane was ruled out with a thigh injury.

FRANCE

DENMARK

SENEGAL

URUGUAY

Pape Bouba Diop stunned France in the opening game

France flop without Zidane

THE LOSS OF A PLAYER of the quality of Zinedine Zidane would have been a disaster for most teams, but France were so strong in defence, midfield and attack that, despite Zidane's absence for the first two group games, they were still expected to cruise through to the Second Round.

However, just as Cameroon had shocked Argentina, the reigning champions in 1990, by defeating them in the opening game that year, Senegal inflicted the same fate on France in the opening game in Seoul.

France hit the woodwork twice but struggled to contain the skills of Senegal striker El Hadji Diouf, and it was his work that set up Pape Bouba Diop for the decisive goal on 30 minutes. World Cup 2002 had its first upset. It would be the first of many.

Suddenly Group A was thrown wide open. Now France were scrapping for qualification along with everyone else. Two goals from Jon Dahl Tomasson were enough to outdo a fabulous volley from Uruguay's Dario Rodriguez in Ulsan, to put Denmark in a strong position alongside Senegal. Then when France and Uruguay played out a goalless draw in their second game, in which Thierry Henry was sent off for a dangerous two-footed tackle, it was clear things were not going according to the script.

Denmark and Senegal consolidated their position with a draw, albeit in a bad-tempered game which brought the dismissal of Senegal's Diao for two cautionable offences.

Senegal clinched their place in the Second Round with a point against Uruguay, in a thrilling 3–3 draw that had seen Uruguay fight back from 3–0

Thierry Henry failed to score and was sent off as France crashed out

"It's been an incredible adventure. The future is ours."

ALIOU CISSÉ, Senegal captain

down in the second half and, in the dying seconds, miss a simple header that would have clinched the points and qualification.

Meanwhile, Zidane returned to the French side for a do-or-die finale against Denmark in Incheon and he looked their best player, despite being obviously less than one hundred per cent fit. Around him the French side struggled for inspiration and Denmark applied the coup de grace with goals from the lightning fast Dennis Rommedahl and another from the prolific Tomasson.

Denmark had won the group and France were out. For the first time since Brazil in 1966, the reigning champions had failed to progress beyond the First Round. And despite the world class strike force, France had failed to score a single goal.

Jon Dahl Tomasson scored four goals in Group A

SHOCKER!
BEATING THE OLD COLONIAL MASTERS
Senegal's shock victory over France was all the sweeter for the fact that Senegal is a former colony of France and all the players in the national team played in the French league. Even the manager, Bruno Metsu, was a Frenchman — probably the only one in the world wearing a smile.

Seoul, 31 May

France 0
Senegal 1
Diop 30

FRANCE: Barthez, Lizarazu, Vieira, Djorkaeff (Dugarry 60), Desailly, Wiltord (Cisse 81), Henry, Thuram, Petit●, Leboeuf, Trezeguet
SENEGAL: Sylva, Daf, Diop PM, Cisse●, Fadiga, Diouf, Diatta, Ndiaye, Diao, Coly, Diop PB

MOM: El Hadji Diouf

Daegu, 6 June

Denmark 1
Tomasson 16 (pen)
Senegal 1
Diao 52

DENMARK: Sorensen, Tofting, Henriksen, Laursen, Heintze, Helveg●, Gravesen (Poulsen 62●), Gronkjaer (Jorgensen 50), Tomasson●, Sand●, Rommedahl (Lovenkrands 89)
SENEGAL: Sylva, Daf, Sarr (Camara H 46), Diop PM, Fadiga●, Diouf, Diatta, Ndiaye (Camara S 46) (Beye 83), Diao ●*, Coly, Diop PB

MOM: Khalilou Fadiga

Incheon, 11 June

Denmark 2
Rommedahl 22, Tomasson 67
France 0

DENMARK: Sorensen, Tofting (Nielsen 79), Henriksen, Laursen, Helveg, Gravesen, Tomasson, Jorgensen (Gronkjaer 46), Poulsen● (Bogelund 76), Jensen N●, Rommedahl
FRANCE: Barthez, Candela, Lizarazu, Vieira (Micoud 71), Makelele, Desailly, Zidane, Wiltord (Djorkaeff 83), Thuram, Trezeguet, Dugarry● (Cisse 54)

MOM: Zinedine Zidane

Ulsan, 1 June

Uruguay 1
Rodriguez 47
Denmark 2
Tomasson 45, 83

URUGUAY: Carini, Mendez●, Montero, Garcia, Rodriguez (Magallanes 87), Guigou, Varela, Silva, Abreu (Morales 88), Sorondo, Recoba (Regueiro 80)
DENMARK: Sorensen, Tofting, Henriksen, Laursen●, Heintze● (Jensen N 58), Helveg, Gravesen, Gronkjaer (Jorgensen 70), Tomasson, Sand (Poulsen 89), Rommedahl

MOM: Jon Dahl Tomasson

Busan, 6 June

France 0
Uruguay 0

FRANCE: Barthez, Lizarazu, Vieira, Desailly, Wiltord (Dugarry 90), Henry*, Thuram, Petit●, Leboeuf (Candela 16), Trezeguet (Cisse 81), Micoud
URUGUAY: Carini, Lembo, Montero, Garcia●, Rodriguez (Guigou 73), Varela, Silva● (Magallanes 60), Abreu●, Sorondo, Romero● (De Los Santos 71), Recoba

MOM: Fabien Barthez

Suwon, 11 June

Senegal 3
Fadiga 20 (pen), Diop PB 26 38
Uruguay 3
Morales 46, Forlan 69, Recoba 88 (pen)

SENEGAL: Sylva, Daf●, Diop PM, Ndour (Faye 76), Cisse, Camara H● (Ndiaye 67), Fadiga●, Diouf●, Diatta, Coly● (Beye● 63), Diop PB●
URUGUAY: Carini●, Lembo, Montero●, Garcia●, Rodriguez●, Varela, Silva, Abreu (Forlan 6), Sorondo (Regueiro 32), Romero● (Morales 46), Recoba

MOM: Papa Bouba Diop

(opposite) Even Zinedine Zidane's return could not inspire the world champions

Uruguay kept their fans in suspense right until the end

Final Table	GROUP A							
	P	W	D	L	F	A	GD	Pts
Denmark	3	2	1	0	5	2	3	7
Senegal	3	1	2	0	5	4	1	5
Uruguay	3	0	2	1	4	5	-1	2
France	3	0	1	2	0	3	-3	1

GROUP B

Spain came to the tournament with a much-fancied team but also a history of under-achievement. Their group opponents, however, looked weak, and Spain were favourites to top the group, with Slovenia or Paraguay most likely to be fighting for second place. Talk of strife in the South Africa camp suggested they would not be a threat, but they would prove their critics wrong in setting up a nail-biting conclusion.

SPAIN

PARAGUAY

SLOVENIA

SOUTH AFRICA

*Raul led a strong Spanish
performance in Group B*

Spain cruise through in style

AS PARAGUAY CRUISED into a 2–0 lead with goals either side of half-time in the group opener, it looked like all the speculation over South Africa's hopes was right. While it had taken a special free-kick from Francisco Arce to breach their defence the second time, they had not looked like taking anything out of the game. But then came the fight-back, spurred by Teboho Mokeoena's goal with half an hour remaining.

As the final whistle loomed nearer, Paraguay's stand-in goalkeeper Ricardo Tavarelli brought down Sibusiso Zuma in the box and Quinton Fortune equalised from the penalty spot. It was a shock for Paraguay, but there were no surprises for Spain as they eased past Slovenia 3–1 after

Raul had set them on their way with a rather soft opener.

Legendary goalkeeper Jose Luis Chilavert returned from suspension for Paraguay's second game, but he could not stop the impressive Spanish becoming the first team to qualify with another 3–1 triumph, even after they had gone 1–0 down through a Puyol own goal. The unfortunate right-back atoned for that by going on to prove himself one of the best defenders in the tournament.

Meanwhile, South Africa had moved into second place on four points, after beating Slovenia 1–0 through Siyabonga Nomvethe's fourth-minute strike. With two defeats in two games, Slovenia were eliminated. If South Africa could beat Spain in their final

Teboho Mokoena started the South African come-back against Paraguay

"On this wave of optimism we can beat anyone."

ROQUE SANTA CRUZ, Paraguay striker

game they would top the group, but if they lost and Paraguay beat Slovenia by enough goals, Paraguay would progress at South Africa's expense.

And so it proved, as substitute Nelson Cuevas scored the decisive goal for 10-man Paraguay against Slovenia (themselves reduced to 10 men) on 84 minutes to send them through ahead of South Africa by virtue of the number of goals scored.

South Africa had played heroically against Spain, twice coming back from a goal down, but after Raul made it 3–2 early in the second half, they could not find a way back. Even so, with just over five minutes remaining they were lying in second place, until Cuevas scored that crucial goal in Seogwipo and turned the tables.

A brace from Fernando Morientes helped Spain beat Paraguay 3–1

SHOCKER!
SOUTH AMERICAN SUPER SUB

Paraguay's fight-back against Slovenia was quite a game for Nelson Cuevas. He came on as a substitute after 61 minutes, scored the equaliser after 65, scored the decisive third goal after 84 minutes and was himself substituted after 92. Carlos Paredes, sent off after 22 minutes, was one of the first to congratulate him.

Busan, 2 June

Paraguay 2
Santa Cruz 39, Arce 55

South Africa 2
Mokoena T 63, Fortune 90 (pen)

PARAGUAY: Tavarelli●, Arce, Gamarra, Ayala, Struway (Franco● 86), Alvarenga (Gavilan 66), Santa Cruz, Acuna, Campos (Morinigo 73), Caceres●, Caniza●
SOUTH AFRICA: Arendse, Nzama, Carnell, Mokoena A●, Sibaya, Fortune, Mokoena T, Issa● (Mukasi 27), Zuma●, McCarthy● (Koumantarakis 78), Radebe

MOM: Francisco Arce

Jeonju, 7 June

Spain 3
Morientes 53 69, Hierro 83 (pen)

Paraguay 1
Puyol OG 10

SPAIN: Casillas, Juanfran, Puyol, Hierro, Raul, Baraja●, Tristan (Morientes 46), De Pedro, Valeron (Xavi 85), Nadal, Luis Enrique (Helguera 46)
PARAGUAY: Chilavert, Arce●, Gamarra, Ayala, Santa Cruz●, Acuna, Paredes, Gavilan ●, Caceres, Cardozo (Campos 63), Caniza (Struway 78)

MOM: Fernando Morientes

Daejon, 12 June

South Africa 2
McCarthy 31, Radebe 53

Spain 3
Raul 4 56, Mendieta 45

SOUTH AFRICA: Arendse, Nzama●, Carnell●, Mokoena A●, Sibaya, Fortune (Lekgetho 83), Mokoena T, Nomvethe● (Koumantarakis 74), Zuma, McCarthy, Radebe (Molefe 80)
SPAIN: Casillas, Curro, Helguera, Raul (Luis Enrique 82), Morientes (Luque 77), Albelda (Sergio 53), Romero, Mendieta, Xavi, Nadal, Joaquin

MOM: Raul

Gwangju, 2 June

Spain 3
Raul 44, Valeron 74, Hierro 87 (pen)

Slovenia 1
Cimirotic 82

SPAIN: Casillas, Juanfran (Romero 82), Puyol, Hierro, Raul, Baraja, Tristan (Morientes 67), De Pedro, Valeron●, Nadal, Luis Enrique (Helguera 74)
SLOVENIA: Simeunovic, Milinovic, Galic, Knavs, Novak (Gajser 77), Ceh A, Osterc (Cimirotic● 57), Zahovic (Acimovic 63), Pavlin, Rudonja, Karic●

MOM: Raul

Daegu, 8 June

South Africa 1
Nomvethe 4

Slovenia 0

SOUTH AFRICA: Arendse, Nzama, Carnell, Mokoena A, Sibaya, Fortune (Pule 84), Mokoena T, Nomvethe (Buckley 71), Zuma, McCarthy (Koumantarakis 80), Radebe●
SLOVENIA: Simeunovic, Milinovic●, Vugdalic●, Knavs (Bulajic 60), Novak, Ceh A●, Pavlin●, Rudonja, Acimovic (Ceh N 60), Karic, Cimirotic (Osterc 41)

MOM: Quinton Fortune

Seogwipo, 12 June

Slovenia 1
Acimovic 46

Paraguay 3
Cuevas 65 84, Campos 73

SLOVENIA: Dabanovic, Milinovic● Zeljko, Novak, Ceh A, Osterc (Tiganj 77), Pavlin● (Rudonja 40●), Tavcar, Acimovic (Ceh N 62✳), Karic●, Cimirotic, Bulajic
PARAGUAY: Chilavert, Arce, Gamarra, Ayala, Alvarenga (Campos 53), Santa Cruz, Acuna, Paredes ●✳, Caceres, Cardozo (Cuevas 61) (Franco 92), Caniza

MOM: Nelson Cuevas

(opposite) Raul sent the Bafana Bafana home with the winner in Daejon

Lucas Radebe heads home the second equaliser against Spain

Final Table   GROUP B

	P	W	D	L	F	A	GD	Pts
Spain	3	3	0	0	9	4	5	9
Paraguay	3	1	1	1	6	6	0	4
South Africa	3	1	1	1	5	5	0	4
Slovenia	3	0	0	3	2	7	-5	0

Brazil couldn't have asked for an easier group. Following an inconsistent qualifying campaign, they came into the tournament in the unfamiliar position of not being favourites, but one look at the group opposition suggested they would make the Second Round without a struggle. China were making their World Cup debut and Costa Rica had defensive frailties, leaving Turkey as the team most likely to finish second.

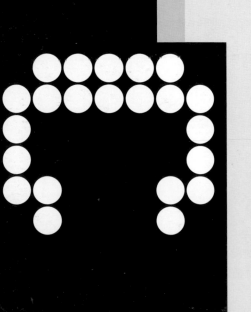

BRAZIL

TURKEY

COSTA RICA

CHINA

*Edmilson (left) admires his over-
head kick against Costa Rica*

Brazil's show of tainted genius

GROUP C BEGAN with signs that another upset was on the cards when Turkey took the lead against Brazil on the stroke of half-time in Ulsan. And although Brazil hit back soon after the break with Ronaldo scoring the equaliser, they struggled to break down the Turks until late in the game.

A penalty was awarded despite the foul being commited outside the box, and Alpay was sent off, leaving Rivaldo to clinch the points from the spot with 87 minutes on the clock.

But the drama didn't end there. The Brazilian hero disgraced himself with a piece of play-acting that got Hakan Unsal sent off. Unsal kicked the ball at Rivaldo as he waited to take a corner and hit him on the knee. Rivaldo collapsed to the floor clutching his face, but television showed clearly that the ball had not hit him there.

After that it seemed nothing could go wrong for Brazil. In their next game they put four past China, who had already lost their first ever World Cup match 2–0 to Costa Rica and were now out of the tournament. Costa Rica and Turkey drew 1–1, leaving the former needing to hold Brazil to a draw or at least restirict the margin of defeat. It was never on the cards.

Costa Rica and Brazil played out a game so full of goalscoring chances and defensive errors that it could have been 4–3 to Costa Rica at half-time, had they been able to head the ball straight. Instead, they had missed a

Hasan Sas struck
the opener for
Turkey against Brazil

"Obviously I exaggerated the incident for the guy to be sent off."

RIVALDO, Brazil striker

series of gilt-edged chances and Brazil went in 3–1 up. The second half continued in the same vein, full of attacking endeavour and scant regard for defence and Brazil eventually ran out 5–2 winners, leaving Costa Rica to lick their wounds and gaze sadly in the direction of Seoul, where Turkey were cruising to a 3–0 victory over China that would put them comfortably through to the Second Round.

So Brazil had fulfilled their promise of free-scoring football, Turkey had pipped Costa Rica and China had gone home from their first World Cup with nothing. But they were in good company: in failing to score, they had matched the achievements of the defending champions.

Paulo Wanchope
bemuses the
Chinese defence

SHOCKER!

GETTING AWAY WITH IT

Rivaldo received a pathetic £5,000 fine for the histrionics that brought about the dismissal of Hakan Unsal. In a tournament where referees had been instructed to clamp down on play-acting, and indeed had done so very effectively, it seemed a poor response by FIFA to allow him to avoid suspension.

Ulsan, 3 June

Brazil 2
Ronaldo 50, Rivaldo 87 (pen)

Turkey 1
Sas 45

BRAZIL: Marcos, Cafu, Lucio, Junior, Edmilson, Roberto Carlos, Gilberto Silva, Ronaldo (Luizao 73), Rivaldo, Ronaldinho (Denilson● 67), Juninho (Vampeta 72)
TURKEY: Rustu, Bulent (Davala 66), Fatih●, Alpay✳, Tugay (Erdem 88), Sukur, Basturk (Mansiz 66), Sas, Umit, Unsal●✳, Emre B

MOM: Ronaldo

Seogwipo, 8 June

Brazil 4
Roberto Carlos 15, Rivaldo 32, Ronaldinho 45 (pen), Ronaldo 55

China 0

BRAZIL: Marcos, Cafu, Lucio, Roque Junior●, Roberto Carlos, Gilberto Silva, Ronaldo (Edilson 72), Rivaldo, Ronaldinho● (Denilson 46), Anderson Polga, Juninho (Ricardinho 70)
CHINA: Jiang Jin, Wu Chengying, Li Tie, Ma Mingyu (Yang Pu 62), Hao Haidong (Qu Bo 75), Li Weifeng, Zhao Junzhe, Du Wei, Li Xiaopeng, Qi Hong (Shao Jiayi 66), Xu Yunlong

MOM: Roberto Carlos

Suwon, 13 June

Costa Rica 2
Wanchope 39, Gomez 56

Brazil 5
Ronaldo 10 13, Edmilson 38, Rivaldo 62, Junior 64

COSTA RICA: Lonnis, Marin, Wright, Martinez (Parks 74), Lopez, Solis (Fonseca 65), Wanchope, Centeno, Gomez, Wallace (Bryce 46), Castro
BRAZIL: Marcos, Cafu●, Lucio, Edmilson, Gilberto Silva, Ronaldo, Rivaldo (Kaka 72), Anderson Polga, Junior, Juninho (Ricardinho 61), Edilson (Kleberson 57)

MOM: Junior

Gwangju, 4 June

China 0

Costa Rica 2
Gomez 61, Wright 65

CHINA: Pr Jiang Jin, Wu Chengying, Fan Zhiyi (Yu Genwei 74), Sun Jihai (Qu Bo 26), Li Tie●, Ma Mingyu, Hao Haidong, Li Weifeng, Li Xiaopeng●, Yang Chen (Su Maozhen 66), Xu Yunlong●
COSTA RICA: Lonnis, Marin●, Wright, Martinez, Fonseca (Medford 57), Solis●, Wanchope (Lopez 80), Centeno●, Gomez●, Wallace (Bryce 70), Castro

MOM: Ronald Gomez

Incheon, 9 June

Costa Rica 1
Parks 86

Turkey 1
Emre B 56

COSTA RICA: Lonnis, Marin, Wright, Martinez●, Lopez (Parks 77), Solis, Wanchope, Centeno (Medford 66), Gomez, Wallace (Bryce 77), Castro●
TURKEY: Rustu, Emre A●, Fatih, Tugay● (Erdem 88), Sukur (Mansiz 75), Basturk (Nihat 79), Sas, Umit, Ergun, Emre B●, Davala

MOM: Paulo Wanchope

Seoul, 13 June

Turkey 3
Sas 6, Bulent 9, Davala 85

China 0

TURKEY: Rustu (Omer 35), Emre A●, Bulent, Fatih, Tugay (Tayfur 84), Sukur, Basturk (Mansiz 70), Sas●, Unsal, Emre B●, Davala
CHINA Jiang Ji, Yang Pu●, Wu Chengying (Shao Jiayi✳ 46), Li Tie, Hao Haidong (Qu Bo 73), Li Weifeng●, Zhao Junzhe, Du Wei, Li Xiaopeng, Yang Chen (Yu Genwei 73), Xu Yunlong

MOM: Hasan Sas

(opposite) Ronaldo returned to the World Cup with a goal in each group game

Juninho battles past Costa Rica's influential Ronald Gomez

Final Table GROUP C	P	W	D	L	F	A	GD	Pts
Brazil	3	3	0	0	11	3	8	9
Turkey	3	1	1	1	5	3	2	4
Costa Rica	3	1	1	1	5	6	-1	4
China	3	0	0	3	0	9	-9	0

This looked to be an easy group for Portugal, boasting World Player of the Year Luis Figo and a wealth of other talent. Of the other teams in the group, Poland were expected to come out on top, although nobody could tell just what effect the fanatical home support woud have on co-hosts South Korea. The USA team, whose exploits, by contrast, would go largely unnoticed back home, were not expected to progress.

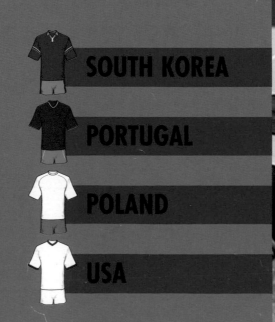

SOUTH KOREA

PORTUGAL

POLAND

USA

Vitor Baia and his defenders can't keep out USA's John O'Brien

Underdogs go marching on

RIGHT FROM THE START the form book was thrown away and the experts had to revise their opinions of South Korea and the USA. The Koreans, managed by the expert Dutch coach Guus Hiddink, showed themselves to be phenomenally fit and resilient as they kicked off the group with a 2–0 win over Poland.

A bigger shock, however, came in Suwon, where the USA went 3–0 up against Portugal and held on to win 3–2. It was as many goals as the USA had scored in three games at France 98, but their attacking play, making use of quick wingers and deadly crossing, fully merited the win.

Portugal stamped some authority back on the group in their next game, sweeping aside an abject-looking Poland to win 4–0, including a hat-trick for Pauleta, but we were yet to see the true brilliance of Luis Figo, who looked short of fitness.

Clint Mathis gave the USA the lead against South Korea after 24 minutes, but the co-hosts piled on the pressure and had a penalty saved by Brad Friedel, but got a deserved equaliser through golden boy Ahn Jung Hwan to share the spoils and leave both teams in with a good chance of qualifying.

Given Poland's form so far, the USA were expected to win easily, while South Korea needed just a draw with Portugal to be sure of qualifying ahead of them. Sure enough, it was South Korea and USA who did qualify, but not in the expected manner. Poland, already eliminated, decided to

Welcome to Korea! The hosts' hospitality kept everybody smiling

"I am very, very happy. To be honest, I'm exhausted, but I'm very happy."

GUUS HIDDINK, manager South Korea

put on a show and beat the USA 3–1, having gone 2–0 up within the first five minutes. That meant a draw would have been enough for Portugal to go through, but they were outmuscled by Hiddink's energetic Koreans and lost 1–0, yet another upset in this extraordinary tournament. What's more, they had Joao Pinto and Beto sent off and Figo hit the post in the dying seconds.

South Korea were group winners, a feat which triggered mass celebrations in the streets of Seoul. Before the tournament there were fears that the hosts would go out early, bringing about a massive loss of interest among home supporters. Such worries could not have been more unfounded, as millions of red-shirted fans turned out to salute their heroes' achievement.

Clint Mathis draws
first blood
against South Korea

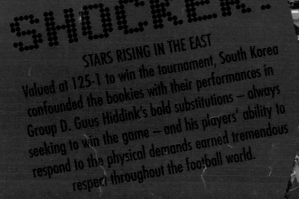

SHOCKER!

STARS RISING IN THE EAST

Valued at 125-1 to win the tournament, South Korea confounded the bookies with their performances in Group D. Guus Hiddink's bold substitutions – always seeking to win the game – and his players' ability to respond to the physical demands earned tremendous respect throughout the football world.

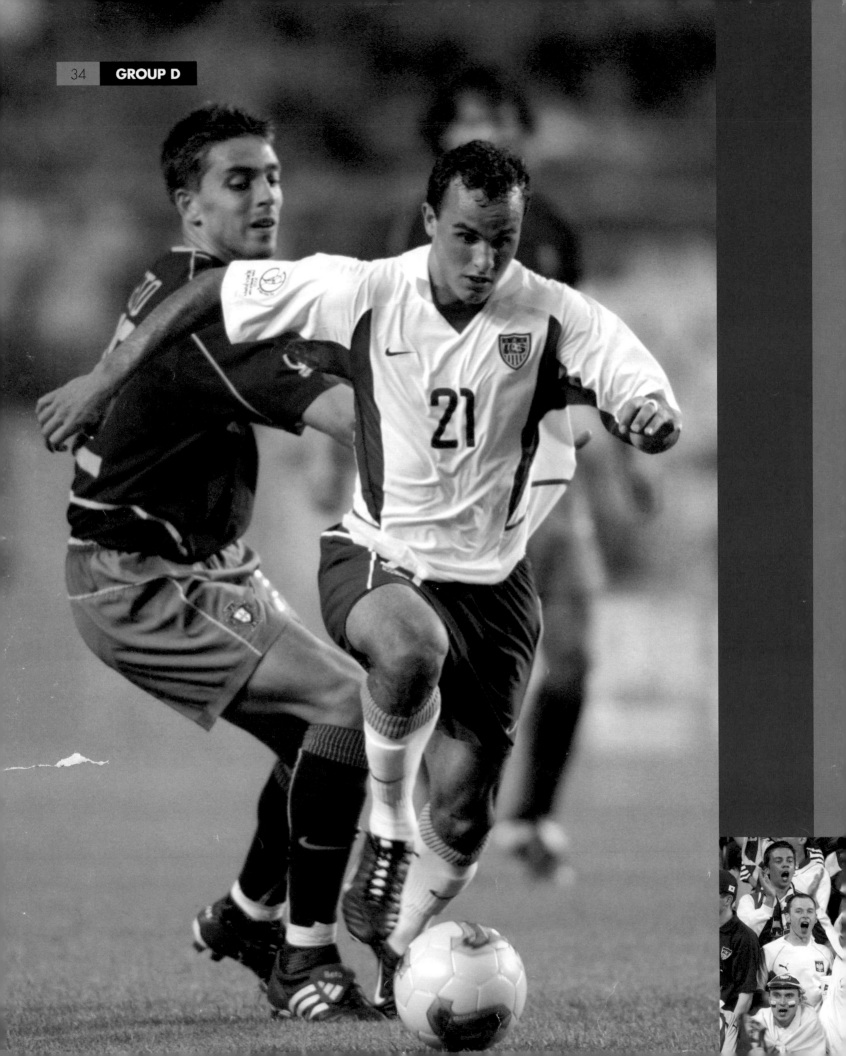

Busan, 4 June

Korea Republic 2
Hwang Sun Hong 26, Yoo Sang Chul 53

Poland 0

KOREA: Lee Woon Jae, Choi Jin Cheul, Kim Nam Il, Yoo Sang Chul (Lee Chun Soo 61), Kim Tae Young, Seol Ki Hyeon (Cha Doo Ri●89), Lee Eul Yong, Hwang Sun Hong (Ahn Jung Hwan 50), Hong Myung Bo, Park Ji Sung●, Song Chong Gug
POLAND: Dudek, Zewlakow, Hajto●, Swierczewski●, Kaluzny (Zewlakow 64), Olisadebe, Waldoch, Krzynowek, Zurawski (Kryszalowicz●46), Bak (Klos 50), Kozminski
MOM: Yoo Sang Chul

Daegu, 10 June

Korea Republic 1
Ahn Jung Hwan 78

USA 1
Mathis 24

KOREA: Lee Woon Jae, Choi Jin Cheul, Kim Nam Il, Yoo Sang Chul (Choi Yong Soo 69), Kim Tae Young, Seol Ki Hyeon, Lee Eul Yong, Hwang Sun Hong (Ahn Jung Hwan 56), Hong Myung Bo●, Park Ji Sung (Lee Chun Soo 38), Song Chong Gug
USA: Friedel, Hejduk●, O'Brien, Reyna , Mathis (Wolff 83), Agoos●, Beasley (Lewis 75), McBride, Donovan, Sanneh, Pope
MOM: Brad Friedel

Incheon, 14 June

Portugal 0

Korea Republic 1
Park Ji Sung 70

PORTUGAL: Baia, Costa●, Couto, Figo, Joao Pinto✳, Pauleta (Andrade 69), Conceicao, Bento, Petit (Nuno Gomes 77), Beto●✳, Rui Jorge (Xavier 73)
KOREA: Lee Woon Jae, Choi Jin Cheul, Kim Nam Il●, Yoo Sang Chul, Kim Tae Young●, Seol Ki Hyeon●, Lee Young Pyo, Ahn Jung Hwan● (Lee Chun Soo 90), Hong Myung Bo, Park Ji Sung, Song Chong Gug
MOM: Park Ji Sung

Suwon, 5 June

USA 3
O'Brien 4, Costa OG 30, McBride 36

Portugal 2
Beto 39, Agoos OG 71

USA: Friedel, Hejduk, Mastroeni, O'Brien, Stewart (Jones 46), Agoos, Beasley●, McBride, Donovan (Moore 75), Sanneh, Pope (Llamosa 80)
PORTUGAL: Baia, Costa (Andrade 74), Couto, Figo, Joao Pinto, Pauleta, Rui Costa (Nuno Gomes 80), Conceicao, Petit●, Beto●, Rui Jorge (Bento 69)
MOM: Brian McBride

Jeonju, 10 June

Portugal 4
Pauleta 14 65 77, Rui Costa 88

Poland 0

PORTUGAL: Baia, Costa●, Couto, Figo, Joao Pinto (Rui Costa 60), Pauleta, Conceicao (Capucho 69), Bento, Frechaut (Beto 63), Petit, Rui Jorge●
POLAND: Dudek, Zewlakow (Rzasa 71), Hajto, Swierczewski●, Kryszalowicz, Kaluzny (Bak● 16), Olisadebe, Waldoch, Krzynowek, Zurawski (Zewlakow 56), Kozminski
MOM: Pauleta

Daejon, 14 June

Poland 3
Olisadebe 3, Kryszalowicz 5, Zewlakow 66

USA 1
Donovan 83

POLAND: Majdan●, Klos (Waldoch 89), Zielinski, Kucharski● (Zewlakow 65), Kryszalowicz, Olisadebe● (Sibik 86), Glowacki, Murawski, Krzynowek, Zurawski, Kozminski●
USA: Friedel, Hejduk●, O'Brien, Stewart (Jones 68), Reyna, Mathis, Agoos (Beasley 36), McBride (Moore 58), Donovan, Sanneh, Pope
MOM: Jacek Krzynowek

(opposite) Landon Donovan leaves Beto in his wake

Poland's fans can at last celebrate after beating USA

Final Table GROUP D	P	W	D	L	F	A	GD	Pts
Korea	3	2	1	0	4	1	3	7
USA	3	1	1	1	5	6	-1	4
Portugal	3	1	0	2	6	4	2	3
Poland	3	1	0	2	3	7	-4	3

In years gone by, Germany would have been clear favourites to top this group, but a slump in the quality of their national side, coupled with impressive form from Ireland and Cameroon, made it very hard to pick a winner. Cameroon were African champions and Ireland had qualified ahead of the mighty Dutch. Now it seemed that results against the dark horses of Saudi Arabia would decide the outcome.

GERMANY

REP IRELAND

CAMEROON

SAUDI ARABIA

Robbie Keane beats Oliver Kahn for a last-gasp equaliser

Germany handed a dream start

AS WITH ANY WORLD CUP, climate was expected to play a major part. As the Republic of Ireland ran out to face African champions Cameroon in Niigata in the heat of mid-afternoon, nobody much fancied the Irish to last the pace, especially without their talismanic captain Roy Keane, who had been sent home in disgrace after a row with manager Mick McCarthy a week before the tournament.

Sure enough, Cameroon began the stronger and took the lead through Patrick Mboma in the 40th minute. But McCarthy managed to fire his team up at half-time and it was Cameroon who wilted in the second half as the Irish pressed for an equaliser.

On 52 minutes, a Cameroon

clearance fell to Matt Holland who drilled a controlled shot low inside the post to earn a deserved draw.

Later that day Germany had a far easier start against a Saudi Arabia side who managed just one shot on goal to Germany's 14. Of those 14, eight went in, including a hat-trick for lanky striker Miroslav Klose.

Germany's next game was a much tougher proposition. Despite going 1–0 up in the 20th minute through another Klose goal, they had to battle hard against the resilient Irish. They looked to have held on to secure maximum points when Robbie Keane broke through their defence and coolly drove the ball past Oliver Kahn to earn another hard-won point and keep Irish

Matt Holland struck a spectacular equaliser against Cameroon

"*It was a disaster.
That was not our team.*"

NASSER AL JOHAR, manager Saudi Arabia

hopes alive. Saudi Arabia put on a much better performance against Cameroon, who had to wait until 66 minutes before scoring the only goal of the game through Samuel Eto'o.

With Ireland confident of getting the 2–0 win over Saudi Arabia that would see them through, Cameroon knew that they needed to beat Germany to be sure of qualification. But the Germans weren't about to give up their advantage without a fight and when Klose scored his fifth goal of the tournament after 79 minutes, to add to Marco Bode's earlier strike, it was all over for Cameroon.

Ireland had beaten Saudi Arabia 3-0 with goals from Keane, Gary Breen and the excellent Damien Duff.

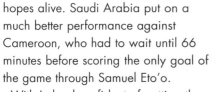

Cameroon celebrate Patrick Mboma's opener against Ireland

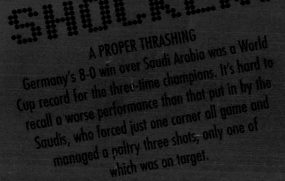

SHOCKER!

A PROPER THRASHING

Germany's 8-0 win over Saudi Arabia was a World Cup record for the three-time champions. It's hard to recall a worse performance than that put in by the Saudis, who forced just one corner all game and managed a paltry three shots, only one of which was on target.

Niigata, 1 June

Rep. Ireland 1
Holland 52

Cameroon 1
Mboma 39

IRELAND: Given, Harte (Reid● 77), Staunton, McAteer● (Finnan● 46), Holland, Duff, Keane, Kilbane, Kinsella, Breen, Kelly
CAMEROON: Alioum, Tchato, Wome, Song, Kalla●, Geremi, Eto'o, Mboma (Suffo 69), Lauren, Foe, Olembe

MOM: Matt Holland

Ibaraki, 5 June

Germany 1
Klose 19

Rep. Ireland 1
Keane 90

GERMANY: Kahn, Linke, Ramelow, Ziege, Hamann, Jancker (Bierhoff 75), Klose (Bode 85), Ballack, Schneider (Jeremies 89), Metzelder, Frings
IRELAND: Given, Finnan, Harte (Reid 73), Staunton (Cunningham 87), Holland, Duff, Keane, Kilbane, Kinsella, Breen, Kelly (Quinn 73)

MOM: Robbie Keane

Shizuoka, 11 June

Cameroon 0

Germany 2
Bode 50, Klose 79

CAMEROON: Alioum, Tchato● (Suffo●∗53), Wome, Song●, Kalla, Geremi●, Eto'o, Mboma (Job 80), Lauren●, Foe●, Olembe● (Ngom Kome 64)
GERMANY: Kahn●, Linke, Ramelow●∗, Ziege●, Hamann●, Jancker● (Bode 46), Klose (Neuville 84), Ballack●, Schneider (Jeremies 80), Metzelder, Frings●

MOM: Miroslav Klose

Sapporo, 1 June

Germany 8
Klose 20 25 70, Ballack 40, Jancker 45, Linke 73, Bierhoff 84 , Schneider 90

Saudi Arabia 0

GERMANY: Kahn, Linke, Ramelow (Jeremies 46), Ziege●, Hamann●, Jancker (Bierhoff 67), Klose (Neuville 76), Ballack, Schneider, Metzelder, Frings
SAUDI ARABIA: Al Deayea, Tukar, Zubromawi, Noor●, Al Jaber, Al Dosari, Sulimani, Al Dossari (Al Shahrani I 46), Al Shahrani AA, Al Temyat (Khathran 46), Al Yami (Al Dosary 77)

MOM: Miroslav Klose

Saitama, 6 June

Cameroon 1
Eto'o 66

Saudi Arabia 0

CAMEROON: Alioum, Tchato, Wome● (Njanka 84), Song, Kalla, Geremi, Eto'o, Mboma (Ndiefi 74), Lauren, Foe, Ngom Kome (Olembe 46)
SAUDI ARABIA: Al Deayea, Al Jahani, Tukar, Zubromawi (Al Dosary 72), Al Shehri, Al Shahrani I, Al Dosari (Al Yami ●36), Sulimani, Khathran (Noor 86), Al Shahrani AA, Al Temyat

MOM: Samuel Eto'o

Yokohama, 11 June

Saudi Arabia 0

Rep. Ireland 3
Keane 7, Breen 61, Duff 87

SAUDI ARABIA: Al Deayea, Al Jahani (Al Dosari 79), Tukar, Zubromawi (Al Dosary 68), Al Shehri, Al Shahrani I, Sulimani, Khathran (Al Shlhoub 67), Al Dossari, Al Temyat●, Al Yami
IRELAND: Given, Finnan, Harte (Quinn 46), Staunton●, Holland, Duff, Keane, Kilbane, Kinsella (Carsley 89), Breen, Kelly (McAteer 80)

MOM: Damien Duff

(opposite) Gary Breen is mobbed after scoring Ireland's second against Saudi Arabia

Cameroon protest to the referee as they go out against Germany

Final Table GROUP E	P	W	D	L	F	A	GD	Pts
Germany	3	2	1	0	11	1	10	7
Rep Ireland	3	1	2	0	5	2	3	5
Cameroon	3	1	1	1	2	3	-1	4
Saudi Arabia	3	0	0	3	0	12	-12	0

GROUP F

As soon as it was drawn Group F became known as the Group of Death. Each team had a chance not only of qualifying but of topping the group, yet for many fans it was all about one game: England v Argentina. Last time they met, in Round Two at France 98, Argentina had won on penalties and David Beckham had been sent off. Now Beckham was England captain — and he had something to prove.

ARGENTINA

ENGLAND

SWEDEN

NIGERIA

Revenge is sweet as David Beckham scores against Argentina

Don't cry for us Argentina

DESPITE ALL THE ATTENTION on England's grudge match against Argentina, Sven-Göran Eriksson, the England manager, knew that their opening game with Sweden (his home country) was of vital importance. Lose it and his team would go to face Argentina under intense pressure.

England began brightly against Sweden and defender Sol Campbell gave them the lead with a powerful header from a David Beckham corner. They had chances to add to their lead before half-time and would have wished they had taken them, because Sweden emerged from the break a different team. They immediately tore

into England's midfield and defence and Niclas Alexandersson picked up a loose clearance outside the England area, to cut through the defence and score the equaliser.

Argentina opened their campaign with a 1–0 win over Nigeria, which was more comfortable than the score-line suggests. Juan Sebastian Veron's deep corners caused Nigeria problems all game and Gabriel Batistuta eventually got a strong header to one of them to claim the victory.

Nigeria were eliminated in their next game as Sweden won 2–1 in Kobe, thanks to two goals from Henrik Larsson, and that left England needing

(below) Magnus Hedman can't stop Sol Campbell's thumping header in Saitama

"It's been a long four years, it's been up and down, but this has topped it all off."

DAVID BECKHAM, England captain

something special against Argentina to stay in contention. Something special is what they got, a 1-0 victory courtesy of a Beckham penalty after Michael Owen had been tripped in the box. Beckham himself could not have dreamed of a more perfect scenario.

Now Argentina, one of the favourites to win the tournament, were in trouble. England and Sweden needed only a draw from their final games, while Argentina needed one of them to lose. It wasn't to be for the South Americans, who could only draw 1–1 with Sweden while England and Nigeria sleepwalked their way through a 0–0 draw.

Paul Scholes brushes aside Nigerian skipper Jay-Jay Okocha

SHOCKER!

FROM ZERO TO HERO

Since his dismissal against Argentina in 1998, David Beckham had been through a remarkable turnaround in fortunes. His wholehearted performances for club and country had won back the hearts of the fans. Now he was captain and his penalty to beat Argentina confirmed him as a national hero.

Saitama, 2 June

England 1
Campbell 24

Sweden 1
Alexandersson 59

ENGLAND: Seaman, Mills, Cole A, Ferdinand, Campbell●, Beckham (Dyer 63), Scholes, Owen, Heskey, Hargreaves, Vassell (Cole J 74)
SWEDEN: Hedman, Mellberg, Mjallby, Linderoth, Alexandersson, Ljungberg, Allback● (Andersson A 80), Larsson, Jakobsson●, Lucic, Svensson M (Svensson A 56)
MOM: Sol Campbell

Kobe, 7 June

Sweden 2
Larsson 35 63 (pen)

Nigeria 1
Aghahowa 27

SWEDEN: Hedman, Mellberg, Mjallby●, Linderoth, Alexandersson●, Svensson A (Svensson Ma 83), Ljungberg, Allback (Andersson A 64), Larsson, Jakobsson, Lucic
NIGERIA: Shorunmu, Yobo, Babayaro (Kanu 65), Okoronkwo, West●, Ogbeche (Ikedia 70), Okocha, Udeze, Christopher, Aghahowa, Utaka
MOM: Henrik Larsson

Miyagi, 12 June

Sweden 1
Svensson A 59

Argentina 1
Crespo 88

SWEDEN: Hedman, Mellberg, Mjallby, Linderoth, Alexandersson, Svensson A (Jonson 68), Allback (Andersson A 46), Larsson● (Ibrahimovic 88), Jakobsson, Lucic, Svensson Ma●
ARGENTINA: Cavallero, Sorin (Veron 63), Pochettino, Almeyda● (Gonzalez● 63), Samuel, Lopez, Zanetti, Batistuta (Crespo 58), Ortega, Aimar, Chamot●
MOM: Johan Mjallby

Ibaraki, 2 June

Argentina 1
Batistuta 63

Nigeria 0

ARGENTINA: Cavallero, Sorin, Pochettino, Samuel●, Lopez (Gonzalez 46), Zanetti, Batistuta (Crespo 81), Ortega, Veron (Aimar 78), Placente, Simeone ●
NIGERIA: Shorunmu, Yobo, Babayaro, Kanu (Ikedia 48), Okoronkwo, West, Ogbeche, Okocha, Lawal, Sodje● (Christopher 73), Aghahowa
MOM: Juan Sebastien Veron

Sapporo, 7 June

Argentina 0

England 1
Beckham 44 (pen)

ARGENTINA: Cavallero, Sorin, Pochettino, Samuel, Zanetti, Batistuta● (Crespo 60), Ortega, Veron (Aimar 46), Placente, Simeone, Gonzalez (Lopez 64)
ENGLAND: Seaman, Mills, Cole A●, Ferdinand, Campbell, Beckham, Scholes, Owen (Bridge 80), Heskey● (Sheringham 54), Hargreaves (Sinclair 19), Butt
MOM: Paul Scholes

Osaka, 12 June

Nigeria 0

England 0

NIGERIA Enyeama, Yobo, Okoronkwo, Okocha, Udeze, Christopher, Sodje, Aghahowa, Akwuegbu, Obiorah, Opabunmi (Ikedia 86)
ENGLAND Seaman, Mills, Cole A (Bridge 85), Sinclair, Ferdinand, Campbell, Beckham, Scholes, Owen (Vassell 77), Heskey (Sheringham 69), Butt
MOM: Jay-Jay Okocha

(opposite) Anders Svensson is the hero as Sweden progress to Round Two

Kily Gonzalez and Juan Veron contemplate Argentina's early exit

Final Table GROUP F	P	W	D	L	F	A	GD	Pts
Sweden	3	1	2	0	4	3	1	5
England	3	1	2	0	2	1	1	5
Argentina	3	1	1	1	2	2	0	4
Nigeria	3	0	1	2	1	3	-2	1

An intriguing group featuring two Latin American sides and two southern European, it was expected to be a procession for Italy with Mexico and Croatia battling it out for second place. Ecuador, making their World Cup debut, were not expected to make much of an impact. But it turned out to be one of the hardest-fought groups of the lot, partly due to a couple of controversial decisions by the match officials.

ITALY

CROATIA

MEXICO

ECUADOR

*Filippo Inzaghi implores
the referee after his late
goal against Croatia
was chalked off*

Mexico are the surprise package

THE OPENING GAME of Group G was watched with great interest to see who out of Croatia and Mexico would gain the upper hand in the race for second place. It was a tight affair, settled by Cuauhtemoc Blanco from the penalty spot after he had been brought down by Boris Zivkovic on the hour. Zivkovic was sent off and Mexico claimed first blood.

Italy were many people's favourites to win the tournament. Exceptionally strong in defence, they also had an abundance of riches to choose from up front. The only doubts lay over their creativity in midfield. Against Ecuador they got off to a comfortable start, Christian Vieri scoring twice in the first half hour, before sitting back on their lead for the rest of the game and cruising to victory.

Italy set about their next game, against Croatia, in similar vein, Vieri scoring again after 55 minutes as they appeared to have the game in their control. Relying on their defence and counter-attacking in small numbers, they invited Croatia to come at them and paid the price as Ivica Olic and Milan Rapaic scored in quick succession to steal the game.

It was a cruel blow for Italy, as television replays showed they had had two good goals ruled out by poor linesman's decisions. But the result stood and now they had a battle on their hands. Over in Miyagi, Mexico continued to impress and claimed top

Ivica Olic (right) takes the congratulations for his equaliser against Italy

"We have been robbed. A draw would have been more than justified."

GIOVANNI TRAPATTONI, manager Italy

spot in the group with a 2–1 win over Ecuador, despite Agustin Delgado having put Ecuador one up.

And so it came down to a nailbiting conclusion as Italy fought for their lives against Mexico and Croatia had the chance to progress against Ecuador. After 48 minutes, Croatia went 1-0 down to an Edison Mendez strike, which left Italy in second place, even though they were trailing to a Jared Borgetti goal for Mexico. However, an equaliser for Croatia would have put Italy out, so it came as great relief for the Italians when substitute Alessandro del Piero scored on 85 minutes to secure a draw and put them through.

For an ageing Croatia team, it spelt the end of World Cup football.

Jared Borgetti's stunning header made the Italians sweat on qualification

SHOCKER!

IT'S A FINE LINE

Italy will argue that it should never have been such a tight conclusion to the group, had the linesman not ruled out two perfectly good goals against Croatia. First he denied Christian Vieri with the score at 0-0 and then Filippo Inzaghi thought he 'had scored a vital equaliser in the dying seconds

Niigata, 3 June

Croatia 0

Mexico 1
Blanco 60 (pen)

CROATIA: Pletikosa, Simunic, Tomas, Zivkovic✱, Prosinecki (Rapaic 46), Suker (Saric 64), R Kovac, Boksic (Stanic 67), Soldo, Jarni, N Kovac
MEXICO: Perez, Marquez, Vidrio, Torrado, Morales, Borgetti (Hernandez 68), Blanco (Palencia 79), Luna, Mercado, Carmona, Caballero
MOM: Braulio Luna

Ibaraki, 8 June

Italy 1
Vieri 55

Croatia 2
Olic 73, Rapaic 76

ITALY: Buffon, Panucci, Maldini, Cannavaro, Zanetti, Totti, Doni (Inzaghi 79), Nesta (Materazzi 24), Tommasi, Zambrotta, Vieri ●
CROATIA: Pletikosa, Simunic, Tomas, Rapaic (Simic 79), Vugrinec (Olic 57), R Kovac●, Boksic, Soldo (Vranjes 62), Saric, Jarni, N Kovac
MOM: Milan Rapaic

Oita, 13 June

Mexico 1
Borgetti 34

Italy 1
Del Piero 85

MEXICO: Perez●, Marquez, Vidrio, Torrado, Morales (Caballero 76), Borgetti (Palencia 80), Blanco, Luna, Carmona, Rodriguez (Garcia 76), Arellano●
ITALY: Buffon, Panucci ●(Coco 63), Maldini, Cannavaro●, Zanetti, Inzaghi (Montella● 55), Totti ●(Del Piero 78), Nesta, Tommasi, Zambrotta●, Vieri
MOM: Cuauhtemoc Blanco

Sapporo, 3 June

Italy 2
Vieri 7 27

Ecuador 0

ITALY: Buffon, Panucci, Maldini, Cannavaro●, Totti (Del Pierro 74), Doni (Di Livio 64), Nesta, Di Biagio (Gattuso 69), Tommasi, Zambrotta, Vieri
ECUADOR: Cevallos, Poroso●, Hurtado, De La Cruz●, Obregon, Guerron, Aguinaga (Tenorio C 46), Delgado, Chala● (Asencio 85), Mendez, Tenorio E (Ayovi 59)
MOM: Christian Vieri

Miyagi, 9 June

Mexico 2
Borgetti 28, Torrado 57

Ecuador 1
Delgado 5

MEXICO: Perez, Marquez, Vidrio, Torrado●, Morales, Borgetti (Hernandez 77), Blanco (Mercado 93), Luna, Carmona, Rodriguez (Caballero 87), Arellano
ECUADOR: Cevallos●, Poroso, Hurtado, De La Cruz, Obregon (Aguinaga 58), Guerron●, Kaviedes● (Tenorio C 53), Delgado●, Chala, Mendez, Tenorio E (Ayovi 35)
MOM: Gerard Torrado

Yokohama, 13 June

Ecuador 1
Mendez 48

Croatia 0

ECUADOR: Cevallos, Poroso, Hurtado, De La Cruz, Obregon (Aguinaga 40), Guerron, Delgado, Ayovi, Chala●, Tenorio C (Kaviedes 76), Mendez
CROATIA: Pletikosa, Simunic●, Tomas●, Rapaic, R Kovac, Boksic, Saric (Stanic 68), Jarni, Olic, Simic (Vugrinec 52), N Kovac (Vranjes 59)
MOM: Edison Mendez

(opposite) Filippo Inzaghi toiled without success up front for Italy

Edison Mendez's strike put Croatia out in the final game

Final Table GROUP G	P	W	D	L	F	A	GD	Pts
Mexico	3	2	1	0	4	2	2	7
Italy	3	1	1	1	4	3	11	4
Croatia	3	1	0	2	2	3	-1	3
Ecuador	3	1	0	2	2	4	-2	3

This was probably the weakest group in the tournament, with none of its teams expected to progress beyond the Second Round. Belgium and Russia, favourites to top the group, were hardly among the European elite and Tunisia had had an unsettled build-up to the tournament with a change in manager. It meant co-hosts Japan had the best possible chance of qualifying, if their performances could match the enthusiasm among the fans.

JAPAN

BELGIUM

RUSSIA

TUNISIA

Junichi Inamoto scores in the 2-2 draw with Belgium

Japan surpass all expectations

JAPAN'S FIRST GAME got off to a sluggish start as they sparred with Belgium to establish a grip on the match. But 10 minutes after half-time, Marc Wilmots struck with an overhead kick to put Belgium ahead and the game came alive. Takayuki Suzuki equalised two minutes later, then Junichi Inamoto put Japan 2–1 up, before Peter Van Der Heyden drew Belgium level with 15 minutes to go. It was enough to send the Japanese fans home buzzing and the point kept their dreams of qualifying alive.

Over in Kobe, Russia went to the top of the table with a 2–0 win over Tunisia thanks to a five-minute burst which brought goals from Igor Titov and Valery Karpin from a penalty.

Then came the shock result of the group, as Japan overcame Russia through an Inamoto goal, scored five minutes into the second half. Now Japan were top of the group, with Tunisia holding Belgium to a 1–1 draw in Oita through a spectacular free-kick by Raouf Bouzaiene.

And so Japan went into their final game against Tunisia on a Tsunami of emotion, knowing that a win would put them through as group winners to meet Turkey in the Second Round and avoid Brazil. With so much to gain, they couldn't contemplate losing and they assured their second ever World Cup win in the second half with goals from Hiroaki Mishima and their star player Hidetoshi Nakata.

Gert Verheyen in action for Belgium in the decisive match against Russia

"This Japan team is like a volcano. I just hope it keeps erupting like this."

PHILIPPE TROUSSIER, manager Japan

Meanwhile, Belgium and Russia were playing out a thrilling match to decide second place. Russia needed to win, while a draw was enough for Belgium and when Johan Walem put them one up after just seven minutes it looked bad for the Russians. But they weren't about to give up without a fight. Vladimir Beschastnykh levelled the scores early in the second half and they went all out for the winner, but in doing so they left themselves exposed at the back and Belgium capitalised with two goals in four minutes from Wesley Sonck and Wilmots.

Dmitri Sychev pulled one back with two minutes left on the clock but time had run out on Russia's World Cup and Belgium took the prize.

Hidetoshi Nakata leads the Japanese celebrations after qualification

SHOCKER!

MAKING WORLD CUP HISTORY

Japan's unexpected victory over Russia was their first ever win in a World Cup tournament. The unlikely hero was Junichi Inamoto, a 21-year-old midfielder who had spent the previous season in Arsenal's reserves. The step up to the world stage seemed to do him good as he scored in Japan's first two games.

Saitama, 4 June

Japan 2
Suzuki 59, Inamoto 67

Belgium 2
Wilmots 57, Van Der Heyden 75

JAPAN: Narazaki, Matsuda, Morioka (Miyamoto 71), Inamoto●, Nakata H, Suzuki (Morishima 68), Yanagisawa, Nakata K, Ono (Alex 64), Toda●, Ichikawa
BELGIUM: De Vlieger, Van Meir●, Simons, Wilmots, Goor, Walem (Sonck 68), Verheyen● (Sonck 83), Van Der Heyden●, Peeters, Van Buyten, Vanderhaeghe
MOM: Junichi Inamoto

Yokohama, 9 June

Japan 1
Inamoto 51

Russia 0

JAPAN: Narazaki, Matsuda, Inamoto (Fukunishi 85), Nakata H, Suzuki (Nakayama● 72), Yanagisawa, Nakata K●, Miyamoto●, Ono (Hattori 75), Myojin, Toda
RUSSIA: Nigmatullin, Kovtun, Nikiforov, Smertin (Beschastnykh 57), Solomatin●, Semshov, Onopko, Karpin, Titov, Pimenov● (Sychev 46), Izmailov (Khokhlov● 52)
MOM: Junichi Inamoto

Osaka, 14 June

Tunisia 0

Japan 2
Morishima 48, Nakata H 75

TUNISIA: Boumnijel, Badra●, Jaziri, Trabelsi, Ghodhbane, Bouzaiene (Zitouni 78), Bouazizi●, Jaidi, Ben Achour, Melki (Baya 46), Clayton (Mhadhebi 61)
JAPAN: Narazaki, Matsuda, Inamoto (Morishima 46), Nakata H (Ogasawara 84), Suzuki, Yanagisawa (Ichikawa 46), Miyamoto, Nakata K, Ono, Myojin, Toda
MOM: Hidetoshi Nakata

Kobe, 5 June

Russia 2
Titov 59, Karpin 64 (pen)

Tunisia 0

RUSSIA: Nigmatullin, Kovtun, Nikiforov, Solomatin, Semshov● (Khokhlov 46), Onopko, Karpin, Titov, Beschastnykh (Sychev 55), Pimenov, Izmailov (Alenichev● 78)
TUNISIA: Boumnijel, Badra (Zitouni 84), Mkacher, Jaziri●, Trabelsi, Gabsi● (Baya 67), Sellimi (Mhadhebi 67), Bouzaine, Bouazizi, Jaidi, Ben Achour
MOM: Yuri Nikiforov

Oita, 10 June

Tunisia 1
Bouzaiene 17

Belgium 1
Wilmots 13

TUNISIA: Boumnijel, Badra, Jaziri (Zitouni 77), Trabelsi●, Gabsi● (Sellimi 67), Ghodhbane●, Bouzaiene, Bouazizi, Jaidi, Ben Achour, Melki● (Baya 88)
BELGIUM: De Vlieger, Deflandre, De Boeck, Simons (Mpenza 74), Wilmots, Goor, Verheyen (Vermant 46), Van Der Heyden, Van Buyten●, Vanderhaeghe, Strupar (Sonck 46)
MOM: Raouf Bouzaiene

Shizuoka, 14 June

Belgium 3
Walem 7, Sonck 78, Wilmots 82

Russia 2
Beschastnykh 52, Dmitri 88

BELGIUM: De Vlieger, De Boeck (Van Meir 92), Van Kerckhoven, Wilmots, Goor, Walem, Verheyen (Simons 78), Peeters, Van Buyten, Vanderhaeghe●, Mpenza (Sonck 70)
RUSSIA: Nigmatullin, Kovtun, Nikiforov (Sennikov● 43), Smertin● (Sychev 34), Solomatin●, Onopko, Karpin (Kerzhakov 82), Titov, Beschastnykh, Alenichev●, Khokhlov
MOM: Marc Wilmots

(opposite) The spectacular Big Eye Stadium in Oita during Belgium v Tunisia

Johan Walem (left) sets Belgium on the way to victory against Russia

Final Table GROUP H

	P	W	D	L	F	A	GD	Pts
Japan	3	2	1	0	5	2	3	7
Belgium	3	1	2	0	6	5	1	5
Russia	3	1	0	2	4	4	0	3
Tunisia	3	0	1	2	1	5	-4	1

WHAT MIGHT HAVE BEEN

WHILE WORLD CUP 2002 will go down in history as the tournament of the underdog, it was also a case of what might have been. Several giants of the game went home cursing refereeing decisions and in some cases those complaints were justified.

Italy suffered more than anyone: their two disallowed goals against Croatia cost them top spot in Group G, and the dismissal of Totti and Tomassi's disallowed strike against South Korea cost them a place in the quarter-finals.

Spain also had a good goal ruled out against South Korea, but would they have even reached the quarter-final had Ireland's Ian Harte not missed his penalty against them, or Kevin Kilbane the rebound?

The USA will ask questions about Germany's handball on the goal line which went unpunished. And then there was the dreaded woodwork. Had David Trezeguet's shot against the post for France against Senegal gone in, would the champions still have flopped as they did? What if Luis Figo's shot in the last seconds against South Korea had bounced in off the upright rather than out? Had Alex's free-kick for Japan crept in rather than rattling the Turkey post, would they have enjoyed the same sort of run as their co-hosts?

It's all ifs, buts and maybes, but it certainly made for an intriguing World Cup.

The Italian bench hold their heads in despair as yet another piece of luck goes against them Right: Zinedine Zidane's injury deprived France, and the tournament, of a great talent

EXPRESS YOURSELF

FOOTBALL WOULDN'T BE FOOTBALL without the players' well-rehearsed goal celebrations. In the opening game between Senegal and France we saw Pape Bouba Diop strip off his shirt, place it on the ground and lead his team-mates in a dance of worship around the hallowed object.

Most spectacular of the lot was Julius Aghahowa, the Nigeria striker, who unfortunately only got one opportunity to display his handsprings. Other players, like Ireland's Robbie Keane, threw in a few somersaults, but couldn't quite match Aghahowa's gymnastics.

You could tell when a defender had scored because they clearly hadn't got their celebration prepared. England's Rio Ferdinand went into a hypnotic, swaying dance, straight off the dance floors of Leeds, and Brazil's Edmilson could only sink to his knees after scoring with a spectacular overhead kick against Costa Rica.

Funniest of the lot, however, was South Korea's speed-skating simulation after Ahn Jung Hwan's equaliser against the USA, a cheeky reference to a controversy between the two countries at the 2002 Winter Olympics.

South Africa's MacBeth Sibaya jumps for joy after his team score against Slovenia
Left: Robbie Keane does his best to emulate Julius Aghahowa

Neuville strike lights up a stalemate

GERMANY 1
Neuville 88

PARAGUAY 0

AFTER ALL THE DRAMA of the First Round group phase, the Round of 16 began in disappointing fashion. Paraguay, who had played with such spirit against Slovenia to qualify from Group B, seemed to have no desire to win the game. And Germany, despite their 8-0 thrashing of Saudi Arabia in Group E, had yet to find any rhythm and flair.

And so the game ground on, with neither side looking likely to score. Oliver Kahn in the German goal had had a fine tournament so far and must have looked like a giant to the Paraguayans, who had their own giant, Jose Luis Chilavert, blocking out most of their goal.

Without Roque Santa Cruz, substituted after half an hour, Paraguay's attacking options looked limited and the only moments of creativity came from the Germans Bernd Schneider and Oliver Neuville. Jorge Campos, on for Roque Santa Cruz, tested Kahn with a free-kick but the game look set for extra-time and penalties, with neither manager making any positive substitutions to try to force the issue.

And then, with two minutes of normal time left to play, Germany struck. Schneider put in a strong run down the right and sent over a low cross which Neuville clipped expertly on the half-volley past Chilavert and into the net. And so the game ended 1-0, a spiritless surrender by Paraguay and an easy passage for the Germans into the quarter-finals.

Oliver Neuville snatched victory with a fine late strike

Date

Saturday, 15 June

Venue

Seogwipo

Attendance

25,176

Referee

C Batres *Guatemala*

Man of the match

JEREMIES
16

GERMANY

Kahn, Linke, Rehmer (Kehl 46), Neuville (Asamoah 90), Klose, Ballack, Jeremies, Bode, Schneider, Metzelder (Baumann 60), Frings

3 Schneider, Baumann, Ballack **0**

PARAGUAY

Chilavert, Arce, Gamarra, Ayala, Struway (Cuevas 90), Santa Cruz (Campos 29), Acuna, Bonet (Gavilan 84), Caceres, Cardozo, Caniza

3 Acuna 2, Cardozo **1** Acuna

England bring home the bacon

ENGLAND 3
Ferdinand 5, Owen 22, Heskey 44

DENMARK 0

WITH SO MANY of the Denmark team playing club football in England, both teams were familiar with what the other had to offer. Denmark, on paper, were little more than average Premiership players, but they had shown themselves to be a strong unit in topping Group A and sending champions France home early.

England had blown hot and cold in Group F, but their defence had come through with flying colours. If they had any nerves about facing the Danes they were settled after five minutes when a David Beckham corner was headed back towards goal by Rio Ferdinand and Denmark goalkeeper Thomas Sorensen spilled the ball over his own line. The goal was credited to Ferdinand, who celebrated with a dance of delight.

Now England looked confident, with the faultless Nicky Butt breaking up Denmark's attacks and setting England off on moves of their own. After 22 minutes Butt appeared in the penalty area to flick the ball on past the Danish defence and into the path of Michael Owen, who turned quickly to shoot low for 2-0.

The Danes looked shattered. On the stroke of half-time, Beckham pounced on a mis-hit clearance and rolled the ball into the path of Emile Heskey, who drove it low under Sorensen's outstretched hands.

Denmark rallied briefly after the break, Gronkjaer trying his luck with a shot, but England looked happy to sit back and protect their lead. The quarter-final place was theirs.

Emile Heskey answered his critics with England's third

Date
Saturday, 15 June

Venue

Niigata

Attendance
40,582

Referee
M Merk *Germany*

Man of the match

FERDINAND
5

DENMARK

Sorensen, Tofting (Jensen C 58), Henriksen, Laursen, Helveg (Bogelund 7), Gravesen, Gronkjaer, Tomasson, Sand, Jensen N, Rommedahl

1 Tofting **0**

ENGLAND

Seaman, Mills, Cole A, Sinclair, Ferdinand, Campbell, Beckham, Scholes (Dyer 49), Owen (Fowler 46), Heskey (Sheringham 69), Butt

1 Mills **0**

Camara puts Senegal in the picture

SENEGAL 2
Camara H 37 104

SWEDEN 1
Larsson 11   *aet*

Date

Sunday, 16 June

Venue

Oita

Attendance

39,747

Referee

U Aquino *Paraguay*

Man of the match

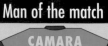

CAMARA
7

SWEDEN CAME INTO the Second Round as winners of Group F – the Group of Death – and had proven to be a match for anyone. Senegal, of course, had beaten France in the opening game and were on a high.

A hard game to predict then, but as early as the 11th minute Sweden took the lead. Henrik Larsson rose to meet a corner from the left and head his team in front. Now we would see what Senegal were made of.

They rose to the challenge brilliantly, El Hadji Diouf worrying the sturdy Sweden defence with his mazy runs. On 37 minutes, he fed Henri Camara, who chested the ball down and beat Magnus Hedman with a right-foot shot. The game continued to swing one way and then the other, Sweden's Anders Svensson going close either side of the break. With 15 minutes to go, Sweden sent on Zlatan Ibrahimovic in place of Niclas Alexandersson and he should have clinched the victory. Winning the ball on the right, he ran purposefully into the Senegal box. He had the choice to set up Larsson for a fairly easy chance or to go for the near post. He chose glory and failed. It was to prove a costly decision.

As the game went into extra-time, Svensson hit a post after Larsson had put him through with a lovely chip. It was to be Sweden's last chance. At the other end Camara scored the Golden Goal with a shot that went in off the post.

Magnus Svensson tussles with Ferdinand Coly

SENEGAL

Sylva, Daf, Diop PM (Beye 66), Cisse, Camara H, Diouf, Faye, Diatta, Coly, Thiaw, Diop PB

2 Coly, Thiaw **0**

SWEDEN

Hedman, Mellberg, Mjallby, Linderoth, Alexandersson (Ibrahimovic 76), Svensson A, Allback (Andersson A 65), Larsson, Jakobsson, Lucic, Svensson Ma (Jonson 99)

0 **0**

Spain survive in a dramatic shoot-out

SPAIN 1
Morientes 8

REP IRELAND 1 aet
Keane 90 (pen)

Spain won 3-2 on penalties

IN THE GROUP STAGE, Spain had been the most impressive team in the tournament. Ireland had shown tremendous determination in coming through Group E and their forwards Damien Duff and Robbie Keane had proven a real handful for defenders.

Spain began well and got their reward after eight minutes when Fernando Morientes headed home. But Ireland were used to fightbacks and set about Spain with renewed vigour. They needed someone who could threaten in the air and 10 minutes into the second half, manager Mick McCarthy sent on the towering Niall Quinn. Duff switched to the right where he terrorised Juanfran and at once Ireland put Spain on the back foot.

In the 63rd minute Juanfran was harshly adjudged to have tripped Duff in the box and Harte stepped up to take the spot kick. But his effort was saved by Iker Casillas and Kevin Kilbane missed an open goal on the rebound.

Spanish coach Jose Camacho decided to stiffen his defences and withdrew first Morientes then Raul. Still Ireland pressed, and in the 90th minute Hierro was penalised for pulling Quinn's shirt in the area. This time Keane stepped up and scored to send this pulsating game into extra time. Without their two ace strikers, Spain were forced to hold out for penalties but they made it through, the exhausted Irish missing three of their spot kicks to Spain's two.

Gary Breen bids farewell to the Irish fans after missing in the penalty shootout

Date

Sunday, 16 June

Venue

Suwon

Attendance

38,926

Referee

A Frisk *Sweden*

Man of the match

CASILLAS
1

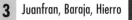 **SPAIN**

Casillas, Juanfran, Helguera, Puyol, Hierro, Raul (Luque 80), Baraja, Morientes (Albelda 72), De Pedro (Mendieta 66), Valeron, Luis Enrique

3 Juanfran, Baraja, Hierro **0**

 REP IRELAND

Given, Finnan, Harte (Connolly 82), Staunton (Cunningham 50), Holland, Duff, Keane, Kilbane, Kinsella, Breen, Kelly (Quinn 55)

0 **0**

Here comes McBride on America's big day

USA 2
McBride 8, Donovan 65

MEXICO 0

Date

Monday, 17 June

Venue

Jeonju

Attendance

36,380

Referee

V Melo Pereira *Portugal*

Man of the match

DONOVAN 21

BOTH THE USA AND MEXICO had surprised everybody with their First Round performances and now the American neighbours prepared to go head to head in a bid for the quarter-finals. It promised to be an exciting game. The USA had embraced wing play, attacking at pace and delivering dangerous crosses into the box. Mexico also liked to use the flanks but could go through the middle too.

USA got off to a dream start when Brian McBride finished off a great run by Claudio Reyna with a well struck shot. Now they knew Mexico had to come at them in numbers and they could hit back with their quick counter-attacks.

Coach Javier Aguirre sent on striker Luis Hernandez in the 28th minute but the USA defence, taking confidence from the goalkeeping of Brad Friedel, looked assured in dealing with the Mexican pressure. Mexico became increasingly frustrated as the USA calmly broke up their attacks and threatened to hit them on the break.

Then, in the 65th minute, Eddie Lewis went on a great run down the left and whipped in an inviting cross which Landon Donovan did brilliantly to head in at the far post. It was the final blow for an exasperated Mexico side, who started to resort to foul play as frustration got the better of them. Rafael Marquez, the Mexico captain, was sent off for a high challenge on Cobi Jones, but the USA kept their cool to enjoy the moment of progress to the quarter-finals.

Brian McBride shocked Mexico with a neat finish to open the scoring

 USA

Friedel, Berhalter, Mastroeni (Llamosa 90), O'Brien, Lewis, Reyna, Wolff (Stewart 59), McBride (Jones 79), Donovan, Sanneh, Pope

| 5 | Pope, Mastroeni, Wolff, Berhalter, Friedel | 0 |

MEXICO

Perez, Marquez, Vidrio (Mercado 46), Torrado (Garcia Aspe 78), Morales (Hernandez 28), Borgetti, Blanco, Luna, Carmona, Rodriguez, Arellano

| 5 | Vidrio, Hernandez, Blanco, Garcia Aspe, Carmona | 1 | Marquez |

Brazil ride their luck into the quarter-final

BRAZIL 2
Rivaldo 67, Ronaldo 87

BELGIUM 0

DESPITE THEIR FREE-SCORING performances in Group C, there were doubts over Brazil's defence. Belgium, well-organised but lacking any outstanding flair player, set out to find the chink in their armour.

They began brightly, causing problems in the Brazilian penalty area and restricting Ronaldo and Rivaldo to speculative efforts. After 36 minutes they appeard to have made the break-through when Marc Wilmots outfought his marker to force the ball past Marcos in the Brazil goal. The referee seemed to think Wilmots had won the ball unfairly and ruled the goal out, although television replays showed that he had done nothing wrong.

Let off the hook, Brazil stepped up their game and forced the Belgians to work hard as Ronaldo threat-ened to break through with his powerful running. Nevertheless, Belgium matched them blow for blow until the 67th minute, when a fortunate deflection gave Brazil the breakthrough. A speculative cross by Ronaldinho was expertly controlled on his chest by Rivaldo with his back to goal. He then unleashed a powerful volley which deflected past Geert de Vlieger into the corner of the net.

Belgium sent on striker Wesley Sonck for Jacky Peeters and threw everything at Brazil in search of an equaliser. But their efforts in attack left them vulnerable in defence and, with the end approaching, they were caught out when Ronaldo latched on to Kleberson's pass to make it 2-0.

Another game another goal: Ronaldo finished off Belgium

Date

Monday, 17 June

Venue

Kobe

Attendance

40,440

Referee

P Prendergast *Jamaica*

Man of the match

RIVALDO
10

BRAZIL

Marcos, Cafu, Lucio, Junior, Edmilson, Roberto Carlos, Gilberto Silva, Ronaldo, Rivaldo (Ricardinho 90), Ronaldinho (Kleberson 81), Juninho (Denilson 57)

1 Roberto Carlos **0**

BELGIUM

De Vlieger, Van Kerckhoven, Simons, Wilmots, Goor, Walem, Verheyen, Peeters (Sonck 72), Van Buyten, Vanderhaeghe, Mpenza

1 Vanderhaeghe **0**

Sun goes down on Japan's fairytale

JAPAN 0

TURKEY 1
Davala 12

THE MOOD IN JAPAN was buoyant after their team had not only qualified from Group H but topped it, recording their first ever World Cup win along the way. But in the first knock-out stage their fairytale journey finally hit a brick wall in the shape of Turkey.

The Turks themselves were relative minnows on the world stage, having qualified for the World Cup only once before in 1954, but Turkish football had made great progress in the last decade. In Recber Rustu they had an imposing and reliable goal-keeper and there was guile and skill in attack too, with the likes of Yildiray Basturk and Hasan Sas. Their defence coped well with Japan's spirited but somewhat wayward attacking moves and they created plenty of danger themselves.

After 12 minutes, the mohicaned Umit Davala jumped unmarked to head Penbe Ergun's corner home for 1-0 and from then on Turkey controlled the game. The masked Tsuneyasu Miyamoto was outstanding in the heart of the Japanese defence as Turkey's tricky attackers tried to pick a way through. But it was Japan's attack that needed inspiration and too often their passing let them down. Late in the first half, Santos appeared to have beaten Rustu but his free-kick canoned off the woodwork to safety. That was as close as Japan came to levelling the scores and as the game went on Turkey looked the more likely to score as they ran out comfortable winners.

The Japanese fans were left in tears, but this was their most successful World Cup and in getting to the second round they had exceeded all expectations.

Umit Davala shattered the hosts' World Cup dreams

Date

Tuesday, 18 June

Venue

Miyagi

Attendance

45,666

Referee

P Collina *Italy*

Man of the match

ALPAY
5

JAPAN

Narazaki, Matsuda, Inamoto (Suzuki 46), Nakata H, Nishizawa, Santos (Ichikawa 46) (Morishima 86), Nakata K, Miyamoto, Ono, Myojin, Toda

| 1 | Toda | 0 |

TURKEY

Rustu, Bulent, Fatih, Alpay, Tugay, Sukur, Basturk (Mansiz 90), Sas (Havutcu 85), Ergun, Unsal, Davala (Kahveci 74)

| 3 | Alpay, Ergun, Sukur | 0 |

Italy cry foul as hosts soldier on

SOUTH KOREA 2
Seol Ki Hyeon 88, Ahn Jung Hwan 117

ITALY 1 aet
Vieri 18

THIS GAME HAD EVERYTHING. After just five minutes Christian Panucci brought down Seol Ki Hyeon and Korea's golden boy Ahn Jung Hwan was given the opportunity to give his side the lead from the penalty spot. He hit it well enough but Gianluigi Buffon dived low to his right and palmed the ball away. Ahn looked to the heavens; his time would come.

Instead it was Italy who took the lead after 18 minutes, Christian Vieri heading a Francesco Totti corner in at the near post. For most of the second half South Korea barely had a chance and Vieri could have wrapped it up in the 74th minute when he broke clear but hit his shot woefully wide.

That let-off gave the Koreans new hope and, roared on by their fervent fans, they launched desperate attacks on the Italy box. In the 88th minute a chip across the area caught Panucci off balance and Seol pounced for the equaliser. There was just time for Vieri to miss a sitter before the referee blew for extra time.

Now came the controversy. Totti ran into the box and went down. Penalty? No, Totti was shown his second yellow card and sent off. Then came a worse decision. Tomassi broke through the Korean defence and rounded the keeper to score, but was wrongly ruled offside. Fortune had frowned on the Italians again. Up the other end, Ahn rose to meet a deep cross and flick it in at the far post. The gods had been smiling on the golden boy after all.

Guus Hiddink congratulates Golden Goal hero Ahn Jung Hwan

Date
Tuesday, 18 June

Venue

Daejon

Attendance
38,588

Referee
B Moreno *Ecuador*

Man of the match

AHN
19

SOUTH KOREA

Lee Woon Jae, Choi Jin Cheul, Kim Nam Il (Soo 68), Yoo Sang Chul, Kim Tae Young (Hwang 63), Seol Ki Hyeon, Lee Young Pyo, Ahn Jung Hwan, Hong Myung Bo (Cha Du Ri 83), Park Ji Sung, Song Chong Gug

4 Kim T Y, Song C G, Lee C S, Choi J C **0**

ITALY

Buffon, Panucci, Maldini, Coco, Zanetti, Del Piero (Gattuso 61), Totti, Iuliano, Tommasi, Zambrotta (Di Livio 72), Vieri

5 Coco, Totti 2, Tommasi, Zanetti **1** Totti

HAIR CRIMES

THE MOST FAMOUS HAIRSTYLE going into the World Cup belonged to England's David Beckham. The darling of English and Japanese fans alike was instantly recognisable with his gelled mohican quiff. But as the tournament got under way, Beckham was outshone somewhat by the likes of Turkey's Umit Davala, with his severe shaved mohawk (a useful weapon against the Japanese, it turned out) and Nigeria's Efe Sodje and Taribo West with their green goatee and braids. As Brazil progressed towards the final, Ronaldo unveiled a simple shaved pattern, just in case defenders needed any help picking him out. But some of the most flamboyant hairdos were worn by the managers. There were Cameroon boss Winfried Schafer's flowing blond locks and Senegal coach Bruno Metsu's rock star tresses. And then there was Germany manager Rudi Voeller. While his players, barring Christian Ziege, adhered to sensible short back and sides, Voeller stuck with the sheepdog curls and moustache that had served him so well as a player. And hats off to him for that.

Ronaldo appeared for the semi-final sporting this daring look, like a toupee without the rest of the hair

"You talkin' to me?" Germany's Christian Ziege mimics De Niro in Taxi Driver

Clockwise from top-left: Japan's Kasuyuki Toda splashes on the dye; Germany coach Rudi Voeller sticks to the tried and trusted curls; Turkey's Umit Davala wears a road-kill wig; Senegal coach Bruno Metsu sports the 80s rock god look; England captain David Beckham with the Hoxton mohawk

Brazil cruise through after early scare

BRAZIL 2
Rivaldo 45, Ronaldinho 50

ENGLAND 1
Owen 23

Date

Friday, 21 June

Venue

Shizuoka

Attendance

47,436

Referee

RF Ramos *Mexico*

Man of the match

RIVALDO 10

THIS EAGERLY AWAITED QUARTER-FINAL between two great footballing nations was expected to provide one of the best games of the tournament so far. Sadly, it did not live up to its billing. Right from the start, England seemed over-awed by their illustrious opponents, defending deep and kicking away possession. Yet the one time they tried to play the ball out of defence they caught Brazil cold.

Right-back Danny Mills fed the ball to Emile Heskey in a lot of space just inside the Brazilian half. Heskey turned and chipped it on towards Michael Owen, whose run was being tracked by Lucio. The defender got to the ball first but his control let him down and Owen pounced to finish coolly past Marcos.

England had set out to defend deep and hit Brazil on the break and, as half-time approached, the plan was paying off. But in injury time David Beckham lost a challenge on the touch line, Ronaldinho beat Paul Scholes in midfield and caught England's defence off guard, feeding Rivaldo to sweep the ball home past David Seaman.

Five minutes after the break, Ronaldinho caught England off guard again, sending a free-kick over the head of Seaman into the net as everybody was expecting a cross. England were visibly shattered and, although Ronaldinho was harshly sent off for a foul soon afterwards, they struggled to mount a serious threat on Brazil's goal. Playing controlled possession football, Brazil ran down the clock and sent England out with a whimper.

BRAZIL

Marcos, Cafu, Lucio, Junior, Edmilson, Roberto Carlos, Gilberto Silva, (Edilson 70), Rivaldo, Ronaldinho, Kleberson

0 **1** Ronaldinho

ENGLAND

Seaman, Mills, Cole A (Sheringham 80), Sinclair (Dyer 56), Ferdinand, Campbell, Beckham, Scholes, Owen (Vassell 79), Heskey, Butt

2 Scholes, Ferdinand **0**

Mighty Kahn gets a helping hand

GERMANY 1
Ballack 39

USA 0

FOLLOWING THEIR BRUISING ENCOUNTER with Mexico, the USA now faced another tough opponent in Germany, the three-times world champions who had beaten them comfortably at France 98.

They began brightly, using their width to create threatening attacks down both flanks, and in the 17th minute the young striker Landon Donovan brought the best out of Oliver Kahn with a curling shot which the German 'keeper tipped round the post.

At the other end Michael Ballack headed wide from a corner. Four minutes later he got another chance and this time he buried his header past Brad Friedel to make it 1-0. Miroslav Klose could have doubled the lead on the stroke of half-time but put his header against the post.

The USA came out after the break with renewed vigour and caused all sorts of problems for the German full-backs. They were peppering Kahn's area with crosses but the German keeper was equal to everything they threw at him.

In the 50th minute there was controversy. Gregg Berhalter struck a fierce shot which Kahn could only deflect towards goal. It appeared to cross the line before hitting Torsten Frings on the hand, but the referee ruled in Germany's favour and awarded neither a goal nor a penalty.

Still the USA pressed forward, Claudio Reyna trying a shot from just over the half-way line which went narrowly wide. In the last minute, substitute Clint Mathis picked out Tony Sanneh with a beautiful cross but Sanneh put his header into the side netting and Germany had ridden their luck all the way to the semi-finals.

USA midfield maestro Claudio Reyna is held back by Oliver Neuville

Date
Friday, 21 June

Venue

Ulsan

Attendance
37,337

Referee
H Dallas *Scotland*

Man of the match

REYNA
10

 **GERMANY**

Kahn, Linke, Ziege, Neuville (Bode 80), Hamann, Klose (Bierhoff 88), Ballack, Kehl, Schneider (Jeremies 60), Metzelder, Frings

2 Kehl, Jeremies **0**

 USA

Friedel, Hejduk (Jones 65), Berhalter, Mastroeni (Stewart 80), O'Brien, Lewis, Reyna, McBride (Mathis 58), Donovan, Sanneh, Pope

5 Lewis, Pope, Reyna, Mastroeni, Berhalter **0**

Fairy tale continues as linesman denies Spain

SOUTH KOREA 0

SPAIN 0   aet

South Korea won 5-3 on penalties

BOTH TEAMS CAME INTO THIS MATCH having been through gruelling games in the previous round, but somehow they found the energy for yet another thriller. And another controversial ending.

As had become the pattern in South Korea's games, they faced a lot of pressure early on and goalkeeper Lee Woon Jae had to be in fine form to keep out the threat from Morientes. Raul, out with a groin injury, was forced to watch from the bench as the Korean defence somehow kept out the waves of Spanish attacks, inspired by the wing play of the 20-year-old Joaquin on the right.

Gradually, though, South Korea began to come back into the game as Guus Hiddink's positive substitutions got their just reward. Lee Chun Soo had a fascinating duel with the excellent Puyol down the Spanish right and Spain's captain Fernando Hierro was magnificent at the heart of defence.

Just as the game was going towards extra-time, Joaquin cut in to the box and chipped the ball back from the byline to Morientes, who headed home. Astonishingly, the linesman adjudged the ball to have gone out and the referee awarded a goal kick.

Just as they had done against Italy, South Korea rode their luck into extra-time, surviving another close call when Morientes hit the post. But they held out for a dramatic penalty shoot-out in which the only player to miss was Joaquin, who until that moment had been the game's outstanding player. South Korea had won again and millions came out onto the streets to celebrate.

Date

Saturday, 22 June

Venue

Gwangju

Attendance

42,114

Referee

G Ghandour *Egypt*

Man of the match

L WOON JAE

1

✦ SOUTH KOREA

Lee Woon Jae, Choi Jin Cheul, Kim Nam Il (Lee Eul Yong 32), Yoo Sang Chul (Lee Chun Soo 60), Kim Tae Young (Hwang Sun Hong 90), Seol Ki Hyeon, Lee Young Pyo, Ahn Jung Hwan, Hong Myung Bo, Park Ji Sung, Song Chong Gug

1 Yoo Sang Chul **0**

✦ SPAIN

Casillas, Helguera (Xavi 93), Puyol, Hierro, Baraja, Morientes, De Pedro (Mendieta 70), Romero, Valeron (Luis Enrique 80), Nadal, Joaquin

2 De Pedro, Morientes **0**

Turks triumph in late late show

TURKEY 1
Mansiz 94

SENEGAL 0

SENEGAL WERE AIMING TO GO FURTHER than any other African nation in the World Cup, beating Cameroon's achievement in 1990. But standing in their way was a Turkey team that had played some excellent attacking football and, in Recber Rustu, had one of the outstanding goalkeepers of the tournament.

Both teams began in attacking mode, El Hadji Diouf for Senegal and Yildiray Basturk for Turkey looking creative and dangerous at opposite ends of the field.

In the 19th minute, Khalilou Fadiga beat Rustu with a well-struck shot but Henri Camara was ruled offside as he intercepted the ball and applied the finishing touch.

At the other end, a below-par Hakan Sukur missed a good chance when the excellent Hasan Sas put him clear. Turkey had another chance to take the lead just before half-time but Omar Daf cleared Basturk's header off the line.

In the second half, Turkey were guilty of overplaying as they tried to find a way through Senegal's defence and they were always vulnerable to the threat of Diouf and Camara. Camara had been the hero in the last round against Sweden and he nearly struck again two minutes into injury time, but Rustu saved his shot on goal.

As the game moved into extra-time it didn't take long for the Golden Goal to come. Umit Davala broke down the right and fired in a low cross which substitute Ilhan Mansiz, on for Sukur, swept past Tony Sylva. It was a carbon copy of Oliver Neuville's goal for Germany against Paraguay and now it was the Germans that Turkey would face next in the semi-finals.

Hasan Sas continued his impressive form against the fiery Senegalese

Date
Saturday, 22 June

Venue

Osaka

Attendance
44,233

Referee
O Ruiz *Colombia*

Man of the match

SAS 11

 **TURKEY**

Rustu, Bulent, Fatih, Alpay, Tugay, Sukur (Mansiz 67), Basturk, Sas, Ergun, Emre B (Arif 91), Davala

2 Emre B, Mansiz **0**

SENEGAL

Sylva, Daf, Diop PM, Cisse, Camara H, Fadiga, Diouf, Diatta, Diao, Coly, Diop PB

2 Daf, Cisse **0**

A CAST OF THO

BEFORE THIS WORLD CUP there were fears that the co-hosting between South Korea and Japan, two countries with less than friendly relations, would be the source of friction and enmity. At the end, as Brazil celebrated joyously and Germany took their defeat in good spirit, we were able to look back on a tournament free of any crowd trouble whatsoever.

In fact, the fans of the host countries were one of the memorable features of the tournament, turning out in their millions to show their support. But while the red-shirted South Koreans appeared in greater and greater numbers as their team progressed to the semi-finals, Japan's fans adopted teams other than their own and supported them with amazing enthusiasm. When England played, the stadiums appeared to be full of English fans, but a closer look revealed that most of those supporters in England shirts were, in fact, Japanese.

Even so, fans did visit Japan and South Korea from all over the world and received a warm welcome wherever they went. Asia had truly joined football's world party.

Clockwise from left: Not all Korean fans were this beautiful but they certainly were passionate; Japanese girls support their own team for once; the Brazil fans are always welcome; England fans have a laugh and a dance; Irish eyes are smiling; a Senegal fan enjoys the upsets

USANDS

Bitter-sweet for Ballack as he puts Germany through

GERMANY 1
Ballack 75

SOUTH KOREA 0

THE ATMOSPHERE DURING THE NATIONAL ANTHEMS was electric. Here were South Korea, one step away from the World Cup Final, and opposite them Germany, answering their critics, of whom there had been many, in no uncertain fashion.

They had conceded only one goal in getting this far, largely thanks to the brilliant goalkeeping of Oliver Kahn, and it wasn't long before he was at it again, diving full-length to his right to save a shot from Lee Chun Soo that looked to be goalbound. That superb piece of football rounded off a good move by the Koreans, but it was Germany who actually had the better of the first half, dominating possession but without creating any clear-cut chances.

South Korea, as we had come to expect, raised their game in the second half, as Guus Hiddink sent on their Golden Goal-scoring hero Ahn Jung Hwan and Lee Min Sung to try and make the breakthrough. Mid-way through the half, Lee Chun Soo broke towards the German goal with men in support. It was a three-on-two situation but Soo decided to go it alone and was brought down by Michael Ballack, who was booked. It meant he would miss the Final, should Germany get through.

But Ballack had done a useful job in preventing a good goalscoring opportunity and five minutes later he went one better by scoring the winning goal. As Oliver Neuville crossed from the right, Ballack shot straight at Lee Woon Jae, but the rebound fell kindly and Ballack found the net with his follow-up.

Hiddink sent on Seol Ki Hyeon, who presented Park Ji Sung with a clear chance to equalise, but he sliced his shot wide and with it went the hopes of the nation. Germany were in the Final yet again.

Date

Tuesday, 25 June

Venue

Seoul

Attendance

65,625

Referee

U Meier *Switzerland*

Man of the match

KAHN
1

GERMANY

Kahn, Linke, Ramelow, Neuville, Hamann, Klose, Ballack, Bode, Schneider, Metzelder, Frings

2 Ballack, Neuville **0**

SOUTH KOREA

Lee Woon Jae, Choi Jin Cheul (Lee Min Sung 56), Yoo Sang Chul, Kim Tae Young, Lee Young Pyo, Lee Chun Soo, Cha Du Ri, Hwang Sun Hong (Ahn Jung Hwan 54), Hong Myung Bo (Seol Ki Hyeon 80), Park Ji Sung, Song Chong Gug

1 Lee Min Sung **0**

Oliver Kahn is at full stretch to keep South Korea at bay

Ronaldo's sudden impact overcomes spirited Turks

BRAZIL 1
Ronaldo 49

TURKEY 0

FOLLOWING THE ANTICS OF RIVALDO when these two teams had met in the group phase, talk before the game centred around how the Turks would react to the Brazilian striker. Much to their credit, they concentrated on playing their own game and, just as they had done three weeks before, gave Brazil their sternest test of the World Cup tournament.

Ozalan Alpay went close with a header and Hasan Sas wasted a great opportunity when he opted to drive the ball across goal rather than shooting at the vulnerable Marcos from the right side of the area.

Turkey were enjoying the lion's share of possession but it was Brazil who created the most chances. Rivaldo and Ronaldo tried their luck from the edge of the area, catching Recber Rustu at full stretch, and Cafu, running in from the right, unleashed a shot which Rustu clung on to well.

It was honours-even at half-time, but four minutes after the break Brazil struck. Ronaldo collected the ball 30 yards out and turned to run at the Turkish goal. Showing tremendous skill, he held off three defenders, burst into the area and toe-poked the ball goalwards. Rustu, caught cold by the early strike, could only get his fingertips to the ball and it spun in by the post.

It was a lesson to Turkey, who had played excellent football but had shown a reluctance to shoot. They kept pressing but Brazil always looked dangerous on the break.

In the final Turkish onslaught, Hakan Sukur spun on a deep cross and struck a wicked volley goalwards, but Marcos was equal to it, saving brilliantly from point-blank range to ensure that Brazil would meet Germany in the final.

Date

Wednesday, 26 June

Venue

Saitama

Attendance

61,058

Referee

K Milton Nielsen *Denmark*

Man of the match

RONALDO
9

BRAZIL

Marcos, Cafu, Lucio, Roque Junior, Edmilson, Roberto Carlos, Gilberto Silva, Ronaldo (Luizao 68), Rivaldo, Kleberson (Belletti 85), Edilson (Denilson 75)

1 Gilberto Silva **0**

TURKEY

Rustu, Bulent, Fatih, Alpay, Tugay, Sukur, Basturk (Arif 88), Sas, Ergun, Emre B (Mansiz 62), Davala (Izzet 74)

2 Tugay, Sas **0**

New haircut, same old Ronaldo as he sends Turkey packing

SWEATING IT OUT

TWO MEN WILL HAVE TAKEN particular satisfaction from the outcome of this World Cup. Rudi Voeller and Luiz Felipe Scolari, the coaches of Germany and Brazil respectively, steered their teams to the pinnacle of world football in the face of severe criticism. Both men showed a cool command of tactics and motivation as Brazil won every game on their way to the Final and Germany triumphed in all but one.

Guus Hiddink will also have taken immense pride in the way he drove South Korea to a level beyond their wildest dreams. Always positive, he squeezed every drop of commitment and endeavour out of his team.

The strain of sitting and watching from the bench showed clearly on the faces of some coaches. Giovanni Trapattoni showed the full range of Italian expression as his team went out, and Spain's Jose Camacho became famous for the sweat patches under his arms, whether his team were winning or losing. Others, like England's Sven-Göran Eriksson and Russia's Oleg Romantsev maintained a steely outer calm. But in the end there could only be one manager smiling and that was 'Big Phil' Scolari.

From left: While Rudi Voeller (Germany) celebrates, the strain of management shows on the faces of Bruno Metsu (Senegal), Jose Camacho (Spain), Sven-Göran Eriksson (England), 'Big Phil' Scolari (Brazil)

Turkey take third place as Red Army sing farewell

TURKEY 3
Sukur 1, Mansiz 13 22

SOUTH KOREA 2
Lee Eul Yong 9, Song Chong Gug 90

THE PLAY-OFF FOR THIRD PLACE has become one of the highlights of the World Cup. Without the tension of a knock-out match or the Final itself, the players relax and show off their skills, throwing caution to the wind and playing in a good spirit. Action is virtually guaranteed, and so it proved again as co-hosts South Korea took their final bow in what had been an extraordinary World Cup performance.

Turkey started proceedings by recording the fastest goal ever in the World Cup finals, when Hakan Sukur showed his old panache in pouncing on a defensive mistake straight from the kick-off to slide the ball past Lee Woon Jae with just 11 seconds gone. But the fanatical red-shirted crowd was brought to life again eight minutes later when Lee Eul Yong curled a superb free-kick into the top corner to make it 1–1.

In such an open game, it was inevitable that there would be more goals and Turkey duly obliged on 13 minutes when Ilhan Mansiz, starting alongside Sukur for the first time, beat Lee from close range. Within 10 minutes he had done it again, playing a neat one-two with Sukur and chipping the ball over the onrushing keeper.

In the 40th minute Ahn Jung Hwan had a goal disllowed for offside and the game went into a bit of a lull after half-time as Turkey began to dominate. But resilience had been a feature of the Koreans' success and they finished strongly again, raining shots in on Rustu, finally beating him with a deflected strike by Song Chong Gug.

It was the 93nd minute and the final whistle blew seconds later. Time had run out for South Korea, but the Turkish players led by Sukur showed great sportsmanship, picking up the deflated Koreans and walking arm-in-arm around the ground to salute their fans, who were happy to join in the spirit of camaraderie.

Date

Saturday, 29 June

Venue

Daegu

Attendance

63,483

Referee

S Mane *Kuwait*

Man of the match

SUKUR 9

TURKEY

Rustu, Bulent, Fatih, Alpay, Tugay, Sukur, Basturk (Tayfur 86), Mansiz, Ergun, Emre B (Unsal 41), Davala (Okan 76)

2 Tugay, Rustu **0**

SOUTH KOREA

Lee Woon Jae, Yoo Sang Chul, Seol Ki Hyeon (Choi Tae Uk 79), Lee Young Pyo, Lee Eul Yong (Cha Du Ri 65), Lee Chun Soo, Lee Min Sung, Ahn Jung Hwan, Hong Myung Bo (Kim Tae Young 46), Park Ji Sung, Song Chong Gug

1 Lee Eul Yong **0**

Lee Eul Yong wheels away after levelling the scores with a spectacular free-kick

Brazil in heaven as Ronaldo makes classic Final his own

BRAZIL 2
Ronaldo 67 79

GERMANY 0

AFTER ALL THE SHOCKS AND ALL THE UPSETS of this extraordinary tournament, it was ironic that the two most successful nations in football history should meet in the Final. And yet this was something of an upset in itself, when you looked back at the forecasts being made at the start of the tournament. Brazil had scraped through the qualifying competition, way behind Argentina in the quality and consistency of their play and heavily criticised by their own fans for the pragmatic style of play that coach Luiz Felipe 'Big Phil' Scolari had tried to instil. "The Beautiful Game," he had said, "is dead," and it looked like he meant it. Also, there was still a major inquiry going on into the events surrounding the last World Cup Final in 1998, when a mystery illness affecting Ronaldo had cast a sinister shadow over Brazil's defeat to France.

Germany, meanwhile, had been written off as one of the worst teams in that country's history, following their 5–1 defeat to England in Munich eight months earlier. They had also lost to minnows Wales in a pre-tournament friendly and, apart from the enigmatic Michael Ballack and goalkeeper Oliver Kahn, appeared to lack players of real world class.

So here they were, Brazil the four-times champions and Germany, who had won three times, facing their first ever World Cup meeting in the first ever Final on Asian soil. Yokohama stadium was packed and a worldwide television audience of billions waited to see whether Germany, without Ballack who was suspended, could contain the brilliant attacking skills of Brazil's three Rs: Ronaldo, Rivaldo and Ronaldinho.

Rudi Voeller's team took the initiative right from the whistle, playing a positive 3-4-3 formation that mirrored Brazil's own, with Torsten Frings and Marco Bode playing as

Date

Sunday, 30 June

Venue

Yokohama

Attendance

69,029

Referee

P Collina *Italy*

Man of the match

RONALDO
9

BRAZIL

Marcos, Cafu, Lucio, Roque Junior, Edmilson, Roberto Carlos, Gilberto Silva, Ronaldo (Denilson 90), Rivaldo, Ronaldinho (Juninho 85), Kleberson

 | 1 | Roque Junior | 0 |

GERMANY

Kahn, Linke, Ramelow, Neuville, Hamann, Klose (Bierhoff 74), Jeremies (Asamoah 77), Bode (Ziege 84), Schneider, Metzelder, Frings

 | 1 | Klose | 0 |

Oliver Kahn grimaces after his mistake allows Ronaldo to put Brazil ahead

Ronaldo's Redemption

FOUR YEARS EARLIER the World Cup Final
had kicked off amid total confusion. First
Ronaldo had been absent from the Brazilian
team sheet, then a new sheet had been pro-
duced with his name on it. When the team
ran out, there he was, but he looked far from
fit and was bafflingly left on for the whole
game. The story was that he had suffered a
bout of convulsions in the hotel beforehand
but had made a late recovery to be deemed
fit to play. However, theories abounded of
foul play and a cover-up. Whatever the truth,
it had begun a sad, injury-hit four years for
Ronaldo, which only a vintage performance
in the next World Cup Final could put right.
And that's exactly what he gave: a display of
the finest attacking skills in the world.

2–0: Ronaldo strokes home the clinching goal

wing-backs, forcing Roberto Carlos and Cafu back into defensive duties. Working hard in the rain, Germany surprised everybody with their commitment to attack and forced Brazil's defence to be at their best, Edmilson making two vitally important interventions to cut out dangerous crosses by the lively Bernd Schneider.

And yet it was Brazil who, despite their lack of possession, created the clear-cut chances. By half-time, Ronaldo had twice been put through one-on-one with Kahn, Kleberson had hit the bar and Ronaldo again had turned and shot straight at the German 'keeper from six yards. Somehow it remained 0–0.

Germany continued to put the pressure on after the break, Jens Jeremies seeing his close-range header blocked in front of goal and Neuville forcing a spectacular diving save from Marcos, who just managed to palm his 30-yard free-kick on to the post. At the other end Kahn blocked a free header by Gilberto Silva.

There was a moment of light entertainment when Edmilson found himself tied in knots while trying to change his shirt. But he eventually got it right and so did Brazil, five minutes later, as Ronaldo struck. He caught Dietmar Hamann in possession and fed the ball to Rivaldo, who fired in a left-foot shot. Kahn, so assured throughout the tournament, made his first mistake, spilling the slippery ball from his grasp, and there was Ronaldo following in to score.

Germany pressed even harder now, Voeller sending on Oliver Bierhoff and Gerald Asamoah in an effort to apply the finish to their promising attacks, but it was Ronaldo whose finishing lit up the Final again in the 79th minute. Kleberson received the ball from Cafu, whose decoy run then stretched the German defence and allowed Kleberson to play the ball across to Rivaldo. Instead of shooting, Rivaldo stepped over the ball and it rolled to Ronaldo, who took one touch before curling a perfect shot just inside Kahn's left-hand post.

It was Ronaldo's eighth goal of the tournament, a fitting reward for the way he had played and enough to erase the painful memories of the 1998 Final. There was still time for Bierhoff to force another brilliant save from Marcos and Christoph Metzelder and Christian Ziege to waste good chances, but Germany could not find a way back and Brazil had won their fifth World Cup.

As the Brazilians formed a circle to offer up a prayer, a dejected Kahn threw his gloves into the net. After all his magnificent efforts, they had let him down at the most important time of all. Ronaldo, in tears, was congratulated by Voeller and members of a gallant German team, whose positive approach had made this one of the best World Cup Finals in recent memory. Referee Pierluigi Collina also played his part, two early bookings being enough to ensure the game was played in a good spirit.

And that spirit lingered on, as captain Cafu, amid a snowstorm of two million origami cranes, stood on a pedestal and raised the World Cup trophy to the skies.

"I fought for two years to overcome my injury and I am very glad to have scored both the goals and help bring the fifth World Cup back to Brazil."
Ronaldo, Brazil

"It's really frustrating when you make your one mistake of the whole tournament and you get punished like that. It's normal to make a mistake, but it's ten times worse when it comes in the final. Nothing can console me about that – but life goes on."
Oliver Kahn, Germany

"I told the players that they had to be consistent, play well, have fun and win. In order to do that, we always knew that finishing second would be like finishing last."
Luiz Felipe Scolari, manager Brazil

"We've got to be happy with what we've achieved here. We played well at times and we owe a lot to Oliver Kahn, who did some fantastic things."
Rudi Voeller, manager Germany

"This World Cup was very important for German football. We showed it is still alive."
Dietmar Hamann, Germany

Sayonara
Japan and Korea

AND SO AFTER 64 GAMES World Cup 2002 came to an end. The World Cup of so many firsts had kicked off a new era in world football. Asian football was now a force to be reckoned with, while Senegal further bolstered Africa's standing on the world stage. Four continents were represented in the quarter finals, proving football was now truly the world game.

Fears over crowd trouble, terrorism or just plain squabbling between the co-hosts had not materialised, in fact it had been one of the friendliest World Cup tournaments ever. The sight of Japan's Emperor Akihito sitting next to South Korean President Kim Dae-Jung at the Final showed the power of football in healing old wounds.

There was some controversy over the distribution of tickets but all the fans had been fantastic. Those who couldn't be there in person had tuned in on television in their billions. In China, a country making its World Cup debut, their match against Brazil was watched by an estimated 300 million people.

The worldwide audience was treated to constant surprises and, when it came to the Final, a game of high quality between two of the world's greatest football nations.

A fitting end to a fabulous World Cup.

Oliver Kahn stands dejected as his team-mates turn their backs on World Cup 2002

STATISTICS

IN WINNING THE WORLD CUP, Brazil achieved the feat of winning every game they played. And Ronaldo scored in all but one of them, finishing up with eight goals from seven games. Hakan Sukur's goal for Turkey after just 11 seconds of the Third/Fourth play-off against South Korea set a record as the fastest World Cup finals goal ever.
And Germany's Oliver Kahn was the tournament's best goalkeeper, letting in just three goals in over 630 minutes of football, an average of 210 minutes for each goal conceded.

GROUP A

France	0	Senegal	1
Uruguay	1	Denmark	2
France	0	Uruguay	0
Denmark	1	Senegal	1
Denmark	2	France	0
Senegal	3	Uruguay	3

Team	P	W	D	L	F	A	GD	Pts
Denmark	3	2	1	0	5	2	3	7
Senegal	3	1	2	0	5	4	1	5
Uruguay	3	0	2	1	4	5	-1	2
France	3	0	1	2	0	3	-3	1

GROUP B

Paraguay	2	South Africa	2
Spain	3	Slovenia	1
Spain	3	Paraguay	1
South Africa	1	Slovenia	0
South Africa	2	Spain	3
Slovenia	1	Paraguay	3

Team	P	W	D	L	F	A	GD	Pts
Spain	3	3	0	0	9	4	5	9
Paraguay	3	1	1	1	6	6	0	4
S Africa	3	1	1	1	5	5	0	4
Slovenia	3	0	0	3	2	7	-5	0

GROUP C

Brazil	2	Turkey	1
China	0	Costa Rica	2
Brazil	4	China	0
Costa Rica	1	Turkey	1
Costa Rica	2	Brazil	5
Turkey	3	China	0

Team	P	W	D	L	F	A	GD	Pts
Brazil	3	3	0	0	11	3	8	9
Turkey	3	1	1	1	5	3	2	4
C Rica	3	1	1	1	5	6	-1	4
China	3	0	0	3	0	9	-9	0

GROUP D

South Korea	2	Poland	0
USA	3	Portugal	2
South Korea	1	USA	1
Portugal	4	Poland	0
Portugal	0	South Korea	1
Poland	3	USA	1

Team	P	W	D	L	F	A	GD	Pts
S Korea	3	2	1	0	4	1	3	7
USA	3	1	1	1	5	6	-1	4
Portugal	3	1	0	2	6	4	2	3
Poland	3	1	0	2	3	7	-4	3

GROUP E

Rep Ireland	1	Cameroon	1
Germany	8	S Arabia	0
Germany	1	Rep Ireland	1
Cameroon	1	S Arabia	0
Cameroon	0	Germany	2
S Arabia	0	Rep Ireland	3

Team	P	W	D	L	F	A	GD	Pts
Germany	3	2	1	0	11	1	10	7
Ireland	3	1	2	0	5	2	3	5
Cameroon	3	1	1	1	2	3	-1	4
S Arabia	3	0	0	3	0	12	-12	0

GROUP F

England	1	Sweden	1
Argentina	1	Nigeria	0
Sweden	2	Nigeria	1
Argentina	0	England	1
Sweden	1	Argentina	1
Nigeria	0	England	0

Team	P	W	D	L	F	A	GD	Pts
Sweden	3	1	2	0	4	3	1	5
England	3	1	2	0	2	1	1	5
Argentina	3	1	1	1	2	2	0	4
Nigeria	3	0	1	2	1	3	-2	1

GROUP G

Croatia	0	Mexico	1
Italy	2	Ecuador	0
Italy	1	Croatia	2
Mexico	2	Ecuador	1
Mexico	1	Italy	1
Ecuador	1	Croatia	0

Team	P	W	D	L	F	A	GD	Pts
Mexico	3	2	1	0	4	2	2	7
Italy	3	1	1	1	4	3	1	4
Croatia	3	1	0	2	2	3	-1	3
Ecuador	3	1	0	2	2	4	-2	3

GROUP H

Japan	2	Belgium	2
Russia	2	Tunisia	0
Japan	1	Russia	0
Tunisia	1	Belgium	1
Japan	2	Tunisia	0
Belgium	3	Russia	2

Team	P	W	D	L	F	A	GD	Pts
Japan	3	2	1	0	5	2	3	7
Belgium	3	1	2	0	6	5	1	5
Russia	3	1	0	2	4	4	0	3
Tunisia	3	0	1	2	1	5	-4	1

ROUND OF 16

Germany	1	Paraguay	0
England	3	Denmark	0
Senegal	2	Sweden	1

AET (Golden Goal)

Spain	1	Rep Ireland	1

AET (Spain won 3-2 on penalties)

USA	2	Mexico	0
Brazil	2	Belgium	0
Turkey	1	Japan	0
South Korea	2	Italy	1

AET (Golden Goal)

QUARTER-FINALS

Brazil	2	England	1
Germany	1	USA	0
South Korea	0	Spain	0

AET (South Korea 5-4 on penalties)

Turkey	1	Senegal	0

AET (Golden Goal)

SEMI-FINALS

Germany	1	South Korea	0
Brazil	1	Turkey	0

THIRD PLACE PLAY-OFF

Turkey	3	South Korea	2

FINAL

Brazil	2	Germany	0

Ronaldo 67 79

Brazil: Marcos, Cafu, Lucio, Roque Junior●, Edmilson, Roberto Carlos, Gilberto Silva, Ronaldo (Denilson 90), Rivaldo, Ronaldinho (Juninho 85), Kleberson

Germany: Kahn, Linke, Ramelow, Neuville, Hamann, Klose● (Bierhoff 74), Jeremies (Asamoah 77), Bode (Ziege 84), Schneider, Metzelder, Frings

LEADING GOALSCORERS

8 Ronaldo (Brazil)

5 Rivaldo (Brazil)
  Klose (Germany)

4 Tomasson (Denmark)
  Vieri (Italy)

3 Pauleta (Portugal)
  Diop PB (Senegal)
  Mansiz (Turkey)
  Keane (Rep Ireland)
  Ballack (Germany)
  Morientes (Spain)
  Raul (Spain)
  Larsson (
  Wil

WORLD CUP 2002 HONOURS

Winners:	**Brazil**
Runners-up:	**Germany**
Third place:	**Turkey**

Player of the Tournament: **Oliver Kahn** *Germany*

The adidas Golden Ball is awarded to the player of the tournament, as voted by the world's football media at the tournament.

adidas Silver Ball: **Ronaldo** *Brazil*

adidas Bronze Ball: **Hong Myung Bo** *South Korea*

adidas Golden Shoe: **Ronaldo** *8 goals*

Yashin Award for the Best Goalkeeper: **Oliver Kahn**